Transylvania 2024/2025

2024/2025

Uncover the Heart of Romania: Where Every Stone Tells a Story and Landscapes Leave a Lasting Impression.

Copyright © Kristy J. Fierro, 2024.

TABLE OF CONTENT

MAPS

Cluj-Napoca

Capela Greco-Catolică
Sfântul Gheorghe

Dog park

142D

Mart

Iulius Mall
Shopping mall

Aleea Slănic

Slănic

Cluj-Napoca

Aleea Slănic

Pec

Școala Cu Clasele I-VIII
„Nicolae Titulescu"

Grădinița „Micul Pr

Aleea Herculane

Aleea Herculane

leea Herculane 6

Google

Keyboard shortcuts   Map data ©2024   Terms   Report a map error

SCAN THIS QR CODE

1. Open your camera app. This is the built-in camera application that comes with your phone.

2. Point your camera at the QR code. Try to hold your phone steady and make sure the QR code is within the frame, especially if you're using a scanner app.

3. Focus on the QR code. Most camera apps will automatically detect the QR code, but sometimes you might need to tap the screen to focus.

4. A notification or link will appear. Once your phone scans the QR code, you'll usually see a notification or link appear on your screen.

5. Tap the notification or link. This will take you to the webpage, app, or information encoded in the QR code.

Brașov

Turnul Alb
I watchtower
th a museum

Brunch House
Brunch

Mori di Sicilia

La Ceaun
Romanian · S

Brașov

Piața Sfatului

Residence Central
Annapolis
4.3 ★ (588)
3-star hotel

Piața Sfatului
Town hall & fountains
in public square

Hotel&Restaur

Google

Keyboard shortcuts   Map data ©2024 Google   Terms   Report a map error

SCAN THIS QR CODE

1. Open your camera app. This is the built-in camera application that comes with your phone.

2. Point your camera at the QR code. Try to hold your phone steady and make sure the QR code is within the frame, especially if you're using a scanner app.

3. Focus on the QR code. Most camera apps will automatically detect the QR code, but sometimes you might need to tap the screen to focus.

4. A notification or link will appear. Once your phone scans the QR code, you'll usually see a notification or link appear on your screen.

5. Tap the notification or link. This will take you to the webpage, app, or information encoded in the QR code.

7

Sibiu

Sibiu
Magazinul Meseriasilor

Electric Com 3M SRL

Strada General Bălan

Strada Răului

Strada Cibinului

ŞANĂ

Şcoala Charlotte Dietrich

Du Monde
Furniture store

Strada Răului

Cibin River

la

à Caragiale

Gasthof Clara

SC Sirius SRL

Google
Keyboard shortcuts   Map data ©2024 Google   Terms   Report a map error

SCAN THIS QR CODE

1. Open your camera app. This is the built-in camera application that comes with your phone.

2. Point your camera at the QR code. Try to hold your phone steady and make sure the QR code is within the frame, especially if you're using a scanner app.

3. Focus on the QR code. Most camera apps will automatically detect the QR code, but sometimes you might need to tap the screen to focus.

4. A notification or link will appear. Once your phone scans the QR code, you'll usually see a notification or link appear on your screen.

5. Tap the notification or link. This will take you to the webpage, app, or information encoded in the QR code.

Sighișoara

4.1 ★ (2525) 4-star hotel	4.3 ★ (564) 3-star hotel

Piața Muzeului

Michelangelo
Italian

Meraki Professional
Beauty Salon

urnul cu Ceas
lth-century citadel
te & clock tower

Burg Kaffe

Sighișoara

ghișoara

Strada Octavian Goga

Eldi

Casa Sighișoreană
4.7 ★ (670)
3-star hotel

Sabion Sighisoara
Jewelry store

Strada Nicolae Iorga

Strada Turții

Google

Keyboard shortcuts   Map data ©2024 Google   Terms   Report a map error

SCAN THIS QR CODE

1. Open your camera app. This is the built-in camera application that comes with your phone.

2. Point your camera at the QR code. Try to hold your phone steady and make sure the QR code is within the frame, especially if you're using a scanner app.

3. Focus on the QR code. Most camera apps will automatically detect the QR code, but sometimes you might need to tap the screen to focus.

4. A notification or link will appear. Once your phone scans the QR code, you'll usually see a notification or link appear on your screen.

5. Tap the notification or link. This will take you to the webpage, app, or information encoded in the QR code.

Bran Castle (Dracula's Castle)

SCAN THIS QR CODE

1. Open your camera app. This is the built-in camera application that comes with your phone.

2. Point your camera at the QR code. Try to hold your phone steady and make sure the QR code is within the frame, especially if you're using a scanner app.

3. Focus on the QR code. Most camera apps will automatically detect the QR code, but sometimes you might need to tap the screen to focus.

4. A notification or link will appear. Once your phone scans the QR code, you'll usually see a notification or link appear on your screen.

5. Tap the notification or link. This will take you to the webpage, app, or information encoded in the QR code.

Corvin Castle

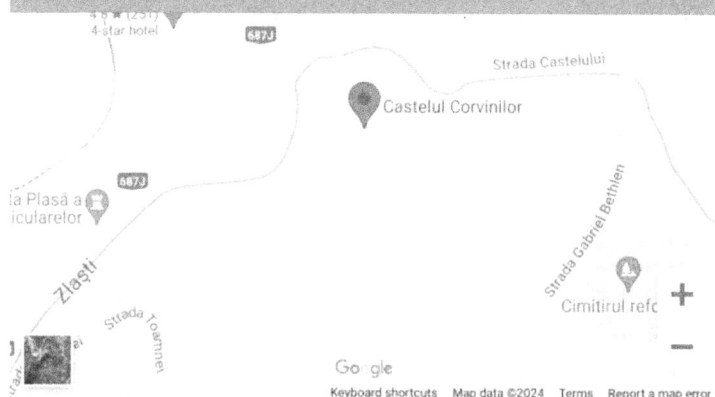

SCAN THIS QR CODE

1. Open your camera app. This is the built-in camera application that comes with your phone.

2. Point your camera at the QR code. Try to hold your phone steady and make sure the QR code is within the frame, especially if you're using a scanner app.

3. Focus on the QR code. Most camera apps will automatically detect the QR code, but sometimes you might need to tap the screen to focus.

4. A notification or link will appear. Once your phone scans the QR code, you'll usually see a notification or link appear on your screen.

5. Tap the notification or link. This will take you to the webpage, app, or information encoded in the QR code.

11

Apuseni Nature Park

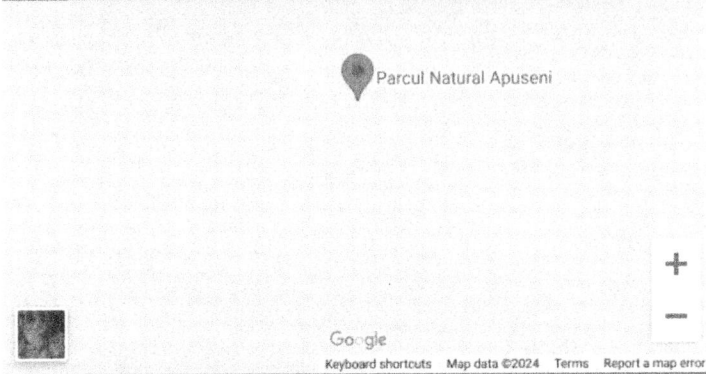

Parcul Natural Apuseni

Google

Keyboard shortcuts   Map data ©2024   Terms   Report a map error

SCAN THIS QR CODE

1. Open your camera app. This is the built-in camera application that comes with your phone.

2. Point your camera at the QR code. Try to hold your phone steady and make sure the QR code is within the frame, especially if you're using a scanner app.

3. Focus on the QR code. Most camera apps will automatically detect the QR code, but sometimes you might need to tap the screen to focus.

4. A notification or link will appear. Once your phone scans the QR code, you'll usually see a notification or link appear on your screen.

5. Tap the notification or link. This will take you to the webpage, app, or information encoded in the QR code.

Brukenthal National Museum, Sibiu

SCAN THIS QR CODE

1. Open your camera app. This is the built-in camera application that comes with your phone.

2. Point your camera at the QR code. Try to hold your phone steady and make sure the QR code is within the frame, especially if you're using a scanner app.

3. Focus on the QR code. Most camera apps will automatically detect the QR code, but sometimes you might need to tap the screen to focus.

4. A notification or link will appear. Once your phone scans the QR code, you'll usually see a notification or link appear on your screen.

5. Tap the notification or link. This will take you to the webpage, app, or information encoded in the QR code.

Castel Daniel (Tălișoara, Covasna County)

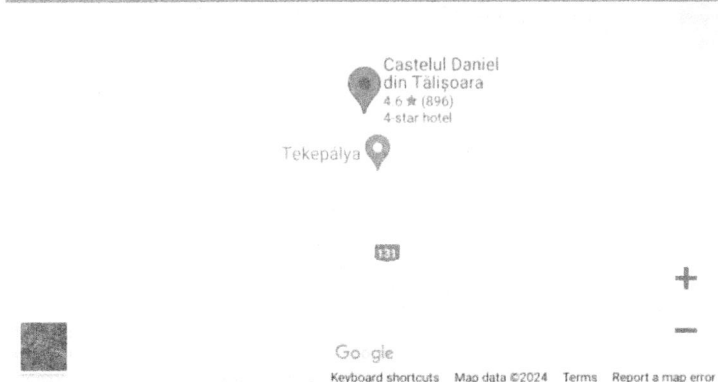

Castelul Daniel
din Tălișoara
4.6 ★ (896)
4-star hotel

Tekepálya

131

Go gle

Keyboard shortcuts   Map data ©2024   Terms   Report a map error

SCAN THIS QR CODE

1   Open your camera app. This is the built-in camera
plication that comes with your phone.

Point your camera at the QR code. Try to hold your phone
:ady and make sure the QR code is within the frame,
pecially if you're using a scanner app.

Focus on the QR code. Most camera apps will automatically
tect the QR code, but sometimes you might need to tap the
reen to focus.

A notification or link will appear. Once your phone scans
e QR code, you'll usually see a notification or link appear on
ur screen.

Tap the notification or link. This will take you to the
:bpage, app, or information encoded in the QR code.

14

CHAPTER 1. Introduction to Transylvania

History and Culture

As the mist rolls down from the Carpathian Mountains, shrouding ancient castles and dense forests in an ethereal veil, one can almost hear the whispers of centuries past echoing through the valleys of Transylvania. This land, steeped in myth and legend, has captivated imaginations for generations, its very name evoking images of vampires, werewolves, and gothic romance. Yet, beneath the surface of these fantastical tales lies a rich tapestry of history and culture far more intriguing than any fictional account.

Transylvania, meaning "beyond the forest" in Latin, has been a crossroads of civilizations for millennia. Its story begins long before the infamous tales of Dracula, in the times when Dacian tribes called these misty mountains home. As empires rose and fell, Transylvania found itself at the heart of conflicts and cultural exchanges that would shape its unique identity.

In the 12th century, Hungarian kings invited Saxon settlers to defend the region's borders, leaving behind a legacy of fortified churches and picturesque villages that still dot the landscape today. The following centuries saw Transylvania become a semi-autonomous principality, a melting pot where Hungarian, Romanian, and German communities lived side by side, each contributing to the region's diverse cultural heritage.

The Ottoman and Habsburg empires fought for control of this strategic land, leaving their mark on its architecture, cuisine, and traditions. Transylvania's position as a frontier between East and West fostered a spirit of tolerance and intellectual curiosity, giving rise to some of Eastern Europe's first printing presses and educational institutions.

It was this blend of mystery, history, and cultural diversity that inspired Bram Stoker to set his gothic masterpiece, "Dracula," in the shadowy corners of Transylvania. While the novel took liberties with the region's actual history, it forever linked Transylvania with the supernatural in the global imagination.

Today, visitors to Transylvania find a land where medieval towns and Habsburg-era elegance coexist with vibrant folk traditions and breathtaking natural beauty. From the towering spires of Bran Castle to the cobblestone streets of Sighișoara, from the bear-filled forests of the Carpathians to the rolling hills dotted with haystacks, Transylvania offers a journey through time and culture unlike any other.

As you delve deeper into Transylvania's history and culture, you'll discover a place where fact is often more fascinating than fiction, where every stone has a story to tell, and where the echoes of the past continue to shape a dynamic and evolving present.

Geography and Climate

Geography:

1. Location: Transylvania is located in central Romania, bounded by the Carpathian Mountains.

2. Size: It covers an area of approximately 100,000 square kilometers (38,600 square miles).

3. Topography:
   - Mountains: The Carpathian Mountains form a horseshoe shape around Transylvania, including:
     * Southern Carpathians (also known as Transylvanian Alps)
     * Eastern Carpathians
     * Apuseni Mountains in the west
   - Plateau: The Transylvanian Plateau, with an average elevation of 300-500 meters (980-1,640 feet)
   - Valleys: Numerous river valleys cut through the region

4. Rivers: Major rivers include:
   - Mureș
   - Someș
   - Criș

- Olt

5. Forests: Extensive forested areas, particularly in the mountainous regions

6. Natural resources:
   - Mineral resources including gold, silver, copper, and salt
   - Natural gas deposits

Climate:

Transylvania has a continental climate, characterized by warm summers and cold winters. However, the varied topography creates microclimates across the region.

1. Temperature:
   - Summer (June-August): Average temperatures range from 20°C to 25°C (68°F to 77°F)
   - Winter (December-February): Average temperatures range from -5°C to 0°C (23°F to 32°F)
   - Mountain areas experience cooler temperatures year-round

2. Precipitation:
   - Annual rainfall averages 600-700 mm (23-27 inches)
   - More precipitation in the mountainous areas
   - Snowfall is common in winter, especially in higher elevations

3. Seasons:
   - Spring (March-May): Mild temperatures, occasional rain
   - Summer (June-August): Warm, occasional thunderstorms
   - Autumn (September-November): Cooling temperatures, less rainfall

- Winter (December-February): Cold, snow common especially in mountains

4. Wind patterns:
   - The Carpathian Mountains provide some shelter from strong winds
   - Local wind patterns vary due to topography

5. Microclimates:
   - Mountain areas: Cooler temperatures, more precipitation
   - Plateau regions: More moderate temperatures
   - River valleys: Can experience temperature inversions in winter

6. Climate change impacts:
   - In recent years, there have been observations of:
     * Increased average temperatures
     * More frequent extreme weather events
     * Changes in precipitation patterns

This geography and climate contribute to Transylvania's biodiversity, agricultural practices, and cultural traditions. The varied landscape and seasonal changes have shaped the region's history, economy, and way of life.

Would you like more information on how the geography and climate influence Transylvania's culture or economy?

Best Time to Visit

The best time to visit Transylvania largely depends on your interests and what you want to experience. Here's a breakdown of the seasons to help you decide:

1. Summer (June to August):
  - Pros: Warm weather, long days, numerous festivals
  - Cons: Peak tourist season, higher prices, larger crowds
  - Ideal for: Outdoor activities, hiking, sightseeing, cultural events
  - Average temperatures: 20-25°C (68-77°F)

2. Autumn (September to November):
  - Pros: Beautiful fall colors, harvest festivals, fewer tourists
  - Cons: Cooler temperatures, some attractions may have reduced hours
  - Ideal for: Photography, wine tasting, hiking, cultural experiences
  - Average temperatures: 10-20°C (50-68°F)

3. Spring (March to May):
  - Pros: Mild weather, blooming landscapes, lower prices
  - Cons: Possible rain showers, some attractions may not be fully operational
  - Ideal for: Sightseeing, hiking, exploring villages
  - Average temperatures: 10-20°C (50-68°F)

4. Winter (December to February):
  - Pros: Snow-covered landscapes, winter sports, Christmas markets
  - Cons: Cold temperatures, shorter days, some rural areas may be less accessible
  - Ideal for: Skiing, winter photography, visiting Dracula's Castle
  - Average temperatures: -5 to 5°C (23-41°F)

Many consider late spring (May) and early autumn (September) to be the best times to visit Transylvania. These periods offer a good balance of pleasant weather, fewer crowds, and lower prices compared to the peak summer season. You'll be able to enjoy outdoor activities, explore castles and villages, and experience local culture without the summer crowds.

If you're interested in specific events or activities, you might want to plan your visit accordingly. For example:
- The Sighişoara Medieval Festival usually takes place in July.
- Halloween (October 31) is a popular time to visit Bran Castle (often associated with Dracula).
- Christmas markets are typically held from late November through December.

Remember that weather can be unpredictable, so it's always good to check forecasts closer to your travel dates and pack accordingly.

CHAPTER 2. Getting There and Around

Airports and Flight Information

Here's detailed   information on getting to and around Transylvania. Please note that some specific details like exact costs and working hours can vary.

Getting There:

1. Airports:
   - Cluj-Napoca International Airport (CLJ): The largest airport in Transylvania
   - Sibiu International Airport (SBZ)
   - Târgu Mureș Transylvania Airport (TGM)

2. Flight Information:
   - Major airlines serving these airports include TAROM (Romanian national carrier), Wizz Air, Lufthansa, and occasionally seasonal flights from other carriers.
   - Flights connect to major European cities; many travelers may need to connect through Bucharest or another European hub.

3. Getting to Transylvania from airports:
   - Taxis are usually available outside the terminals.
   - Some hotels offer shuttle services (check in advance).
   - Car rental agencies are present at the airports.
   - Public buses connect airports to city centers (less frequent but cheaper option).

4. Booking Requirements:
   - Valid passport (check visa requirements based on your nationality)
   - Return or onward ticket (may be required)
   - Accommodation details
   - Travel insurance (recommended)

Getting Around Transylvania:

1. Car Rental:
   - Available at airports and major cities
   - International driver's license usually required
   - Cost: Varies, but typically ranges from €20-€50 per day
   - Allows flexibility to explore rural areas

2. Trains:
   - Operated by CFR (Căile Ferate Române)
   - Connect major cities in Transylvania
   - More economical but can be slower
   - Cost: Varies by distance and class, but generally affordable (e.g., €10-€30 for longer journeys)

3. Buses:
   - Extensive network connecting cities and towns
   - Often cheaper than trains but can be less comfortable for long journeys
   - Cost: Similar to or slightly less than train fares

4. Taxis and Ride-sharing:
   - Available in cities and larger towns
   - Use licensed taxis or well-known ride-sharing apps
   - Cost: Varies by city, but generally affordable by Western standards

5. Bicycle Rentals:
  - Available in some tourist areas
  - Good for exploring cities or rural areas in good weather
  - Cost: Around €10-€20 per day

Working Hours:
- Public transportation typically runs from early morning (around 5-6 AM) to late evening (around 11 PM-midnight)
- Taxis and ride-sharing services often available 24/7 in larger cities
- Car rentals usually follow standard business hours, with some airport locations open later

Routes:
- Major routes connect cities like Cluj-Napoca, Brașov, Sibiu, and Sighișoara
- Rural areas may have less frequent public transportation

Costs can vary significantly based on the mode of transport, distance, and current economic conditions. It's always a good idea to check multiple options and book in advance when possible for better rates.

Train and Bus Services

Getting There:

1. Train Services:
- Main route: Most international trains to Transylvania arrive in Cluj-Napoca, the region's largest city.
- Cost: Varies widely depending on origin, but expect to pay €30-€100 from Budapest or Bucharest.
- Booking: Can be done online through CFR (Romanian Railways) website or at station ticket offices.

- Requirements: Valid passport for international travel.
- Working hours: Trains generally run daily, with more frequent services during daytime hours.

2. Bus Services:
- Main routes: International buses often arrive in major cities like Cluj-Napoca, Brasov, or Sibiu.
- Cost: Generally cheaper than trains, around €20-€60 for international routes.
- Booking: Through companies like Flixbus or Eurolines, online or at bus stations.
- Requirements: Valid passport for international travel.
- Working hours: Vary by route, but many offer overnight services.

Getting Around:

1. Regional Trains:
- Routes: Connect major Transylvanian cities and towns.
- Cost: Affordable, typically €5-€20 for most journeys within Transylvania.
- Booking: At station ticket offices or online through CFR.
- Working hours: Trains run daily, more frequent during daytime.

2. Regional Buses:
- Routes: Extensive network covering cities, towns, and rural areas.
- Cost: Often slightly cheaper than trains, around €3-€15 for most journeys.
- Booking: Usually at bus stations, some companies offer online booking.
- Working hours: Frequent services during the day, fewer at night.

Navigation:
- For trains, use the CFR website or app for route planning.
- For buses, individual company websites or Rome2Rio can be helpful.
- Google Maps generally provides reliable public transport information in larger cities.

General Tips:
- Book in advance for better prices, especially in peak season.
- Always carry your passport for identification.
- Consider a rail pass if planning extensive train travel.

Car Rental and Driving Tips

Getting to and around Transylvania by car can be a great way to explore the region. Here's some information on car rental and driving tips:

Getting There:

1. Airports: The main airports serving Transylvania are Cluj-Napoca International Airport, Sibiu International Airport, and Târgu Mureș Transilvania Airport. You can rent cars at these airports.

2. By road: If you're coming from elsewhere in Europe, you can drive into Romania via major highways from Hungary, Serbia, Bulgaria, or Ukraine.

Car Rental:

1. Companies: Major international car rental companies like Avis, Hertz, Europcar, and local Romanian companies operate in Transylvania.

2. Requirements: You typically need to be at least 21 years old (sometimes 25 for certain car categories) and have a valid driver's license. An International Driving Permit is recommended.

3. Cost: Prices vary depending on the type of car and rental duration, but are generally reasonable compared to Western European rates.

Driving Tips:

1. Road conditions: Main roads are generally in good condition, but rural roads can be rough. Be prepared for occasional potholes.

2. Speed limits:
   - In towns: 50 km/h (31 mph)
   - Outside towns: 90 km/h (56 mph)
   - Expressways: 100 km/h (62 mph)
   - Motorways: 130 km/h (81 mph)

3. Vignette: You need to purchase a road vignette (rovinieta) for driving on national roads. This can be bought at border points, gas stations, or online.

4. Winter driving: If visiting in winter, snow tires are mandatory between November 1 and March 31.

5. Beware of wildlife: In rural areas, be cautious of livestock or wild animals on the road, especially at night.

6. GPS: While helpful, GPS isn't always reliable in remote areas. Having a physical map as backup is advisable.

7. Fuel stations: These are common in cities and along main roads, but can be sparse in rural areas. Plan accordingly.

8. Alcohol limit: Romania has a zero-tolerance policy for drink driving.

9. Police: Keep your documents handy. Police can request to see your license, car registration, and insurance at any time.

Driving in Transylvania can offer flexibility and access to off-the-beaten-path locations, but it requires alertness and adherence to local driving laws.

Local Transportation Options

Local Transportation Options in Transylvania:

1. Public Buses:
   - Most cities have public bus systems for getting around urban areas.

2. Trains:
   - The rail network connects major Transylvanian cities and towns.

3. Taxis:
   - Available in cities and larger towns. Always ensure the taxi is licensed and the meter is running.

4. Ride-sharing:
   - Services like Uber and Bolt are available in larger cities such as Cluj-Napoca and Brașov.

5. Car Rental:
- Available at airports and in major cities. This can be a good option for exploring rural areas.

6. Bicycle Rentals:
- Available in some tourist areas and cities, particularly during the warmer months.

7. Walking:
- Many Transylvanian cities have historic centers that are best explored on foot.

8. Inter-city Buses:
- For traveling between Transylvanian cities and towns, there are regular bus services.

When planning your trip, it's advisable to check the most current information about transportation options, as services can change. Also, in more rural areas, transportation options might be more limited, so planning ahead is recommended.

CHAPTER 3. Top Cities and Towns to Visit

Cluj-Napoca

Description:
Cluj-Napoca, often simply called Cluj, is the unofficial capital of Transylvania and the second-largest city in Romania. It's a vibrant university town with a rich history, beautiful architecture, and a thriving cultural scene. The city seamlessly blends its medieval charm with modern amenities, making it a popular destination for tourists.

Location:
Cluj-Napoca is located in northwestern Romania, in the Someşul Mic River valley. It's situated about 450 km northwest of Bucharest, the country's capital.

How to get there:
1. By Air: Cluj-Napoca International Airport (CLJ) serves the city with connections to many European destinations.
2. By Train: Regular train services connect Cluj-Napoca to major Romanian cities and some international destinations.
3. By Bus: National and international bus services are available.
4. By Car: The city is accessible via major highways from various parts of Romania.

Cost of getting there:
Costs can vary widely depending on your starting point and mode of transportation. As a rough estimate:
- Flights from major European cities: €50-€200
- Train from Bucharest: €15-€30
- Bus from Bucharest: €15-€25

These are approximate costs and can change based on factors like booking time, season, and specific route.

Features and exploring the town:

1. St. Michael's Church: A stunning Gothic-style church in the city center.
2. Piața Unirii (Union Square): The main square, surrounded by colorful baroque buildings.
3. National Museum of Transylvanian History: Housed in a 15th-century building, it offers insights into the region's past.
4. Botanical Garden: One of the largest in Europe, featuring over 10,000 plant species.
5. Cluj-Napoca National Theatre: A beautiful neo-baroque building hosting various performances.
6. Cetățuia Hill: Offers panoramic views of the city.

7. Hoia-Baciu Forest: Known for its folklore and alleged paranormal activity.
8. Central Park: A large green space perfect for relaxation and outdoor activities.

Exploring Cluj-Napoca:
- Walking tours are popular and an excellent way to see the main sights.
- The city has an efficient public transportation system with buses and trams.
- Bike rentals are available for those who prefer cycling.
- The compact city center is easily walkable.
- Numerous cafes, restaurants, and bars in the old town area offer opportunities to experience local cuisine and nightlife.
- Cluj-Napoca hosts several festivals throughout the year, including the Transylvania International Film Festival (TIFF) and Electric Castle music festival.

Brașov

Description:
Brașov is a charming medieval city nestled in the heart of Transylvania. It's known for its well-preserved historic center, Gothic architecture, and stunning mountain scenery. The city blends rich history with modern amenities, making it a popular destination for tourists.

Location:
Brașov is located in central Romania, about 166 km (103 miles) north of Bucharest, the country's capital. It's situated at the foot of the Carpathian Mountains, in a basin surrounded by Mount Tâmpa and other hills.

How to get there:
1. By air: The nearest major airport is Henri Coandă International Airport in Bucharest. From there, you can:
  - Take a train (3-4 hours)
  - Rent a car (2.5-3 hours drive)
  - Take a bus (3-4 hours)

2. By train: Direct trains run from Bucharest and other major Romanian cities to Brașov.

3. By car: Well-connected highways make driving to Brașov relatively easy from other parts of Romania.

Cost of getting there (approximate, as of 2024):
- Flight to Bucharest from major European cities: €50-€200
- Train from Bucharest to Brașov: €10-€20
- Bus from Bucharest to Brașov: €8-€15
- Car rental per day: €20-€40

Features and exploring the town:
1. Council Square (Piața Sfatului): The heart of the old town, surrounded by colorful baroque buildings.

2. Black Church (Biserica Neagră): The largest Gothic church in Eastern Europe, known for its impressive organ and collection of Oriental carpets.

3. Tampa Mountain: Take the cable car or hike up for panoramic views of the city.

4. Catherine's Gate: One of the oldest remaining gates of the medieval fortress.

5. Rope Street (Strada Sforii): One of the narrowest streets in Europe.

6. First Romanian School Museum: Learn about the history of Romanian education.

7. Brașov Citadel: A well-preserved fortress offering great views of the city.

8. Schei District: The old Romanian quarter with traditional architecture.

9. Nearby attractions: Bran Castle (often associated with Dracula) is about 30 km away.

Exploring Brașov:
- The historic center is compact and walkable.
- Public transportation (buses and taxis) is available for longer distances.

- Guided walking tours are popular for learning about the city's history.
- Many restaurants offer traditional Romanian cuisine.
- The city serves as a good base for exploring nearby mountain resorts and ski areas.

Sibiu

(Description):
Sibiu is a charming medieval town known for its Germanic architecture, cultural venues, and historical significance. It was the European Capital of Culture in 2007 and continues to be a major cultural center in Romania. The city is famous for its well-preserved old town, featuring cobblestone streets, fortified church spires, and grand squares.

Location:
Sibiu is located in southern Transylvania, in central Romania. It sits at the foothills of the Cindrel Mountains, part of the Southern Carpathians.

How to get there:
1. By Air: Sibiu International Airport (SBZ) is located about 6 km west of the city center. It has direct flights from several European cities.
2. By Train: Sibiu is well-connected to other major Romanian cities by rail.
3. By Bus: National and international bus services connect Sibiu to various cities in Romania and Europe.
4. By Car: Sibiu is accessible via major highways from other Romanian cities.

Cost of getting there:
Costs can vary significantly depending on your starting point and mode of transportation. As a rough estimate:
- Flights from major European cities: €50-€200
- Train from Bucharest: €15-€30
- Bus from Bucharest: €10-€20
- Car rental per day: €20-€40

These are approximate costs and can change based on factors like season, advance booking, and current rates.

Features and exploring the town:

1. Piața Mare (Large Square): The heart of the old town, surrounded by colorful houses and cafes.

2. Brukenthal National Museum: Romania's oldest museum, housed in a Baroque palace.

3. ASTRA National Museum Complex: One of the largest open-air ethnographic museums in Europe.

4. Lutheran Cathedral: A 14th-century Gothic church with a distinctive spire.

5. Bridge of Lies: A cast-iron bridge with an intriguing name and local legends.

6. Sibiu Lutheran Cathedral: Known for its 7-ton organ and panoramic tower views.

7. Passage of Steps: A picturesque covered stairway connecting the Upper Town and Lower Town.

8. Sibiu Christmas Market: One of the most beautiful in Romania, if visiting in December.

Tips for exploring:
- Many attractions are within walking distance in the old town.
- Consider a walking tour to learn about the city's history and architecture.
- Try local Transylvanian cuisine in traditional restaurants.
- Visit during the Sibiu International Theatre Festival (June) for a cultural experience.
- Use the local bus system for attractions further from the center.

Sibiu offers a mix of history, culture, and modern amenities, making it a popular destination for tourists visiting Transylvania. Its well-preserved medieval charm and vibrant cultural scene provide a memorable experience for visitors.

Sighișoara

(Description):
Sighișoara is a small but remarkably well-preserved medieval town, known for its colorful buildings, cobblestone streets, and fairy-tale atmosphere. It's famous as the birthplace of Vlad the Impaler, the historical figure who inspired Bram Stoker's Dracula. The town's historic center is a UNESCO World Heritage site, celebrated for its 850-year-old architecture and fortified churches.

Location:
Sighișoara is located in the historic region of Transylvania, in Mureș County, central Romania. It sits on the Târnava Mare River.

How to get there:
1. By Train: Sighișoara has a railway station with connections to major Romanian cities.

2. By Bus: Regular bus services connect Sighișoara to other Romanian towns and cities.

3. By Car: Accessible via national roads, it's about a 1.5-hour drive from Sibiu or Brașov.

4. Nearest Airport: The closest major airport is in Târgu Mureș (TGM), about 54 km away.

Cost of getting there:
Costs can vary based on your starting point and mode of transportation. Approximate costs:
- Train from Bucharest: €15-€25
- Bus from Bucharest: €12-€20
- Car rental per day: €20-€40
- Taxi from Târgu Mureș airport: €40-€50

Features and exploring the town:

1. Clock Tower (Turnul cu Ceas): The symbol of Sighișoara, offering panoramic views of the town.

2. Church on the Hill: A beautiful Gothic church reached by a covered wooden staircase known as the Scholars' Stairs.

3. Vlad Dracul House: The alleged birthplace of Vlad the Impaler, now a restaurant and small museum.

4. The Citadel Square: The heart of the old town, surrounded by colorful medieval houses.

5. Weapon Museum: Located in the Clock Tower, showcasing medieval weapons and town artifacts.

6. Torture Museum: A small museum displaying medieval torture devices (not for the faint-hearted).

7. Sighişoara Medieval Festival: An annual event in July featuring medieval reenactments, crafts, and performances.

8. The Covered Staircase: A historic covered wooden stairway leading to the Church on the Hill.

Tips for exploring:
- The historic center is compact and best explored on foot.
- Consider hiring a local guide for in-depth historical insights.
- Try traditional Romanian cuisine at one of the restaurants in the citadel.
- Visit the local craft shops for unique souvenirs.
- Climb the Clock Tower for the best views of the town.
- If visiting in summer, check the dates for the Medieval Festival.

Sighişoara offers a unique glimpse into medieval Transylvanian life. Its well-preserved architecture, rich history, and connection to the Dracula legend make it a popular stop on many Transylvania itineraries. The town's small size allows for a thorough exploration in a day or two, but its charm might entice you to stay longer.

Alba Iulia

(Description):
Alba Iulia is a city of great historical significance in Transylvania. It's known for its star-shaped Vauban citadel, the Alba Carolina Citadel, which is one of the largest and best-preserved of its kind in Europe. The city played a crucial role in Romanian history, being the site where the unification of Transylvania with Romania was declared in 1918.

Location:
Alba Iulia is located in central Romania, in the western part of Transylvania. It sits along the Mureş River, about 170 km northwest of Bucharest.

How to get there:
1. By Train: Alba Iulia has a railway station with connections to major Romanian cities.
2. By Bus: National bus services connect Alba Iulia to other Romanian cities.
3. By Car: The city is accessible via national roads DN1 and E81.
4. By Air: The nearest airport is in Sibiu (70 km away) or Cluj-Napoca (120 km away).

Cost of getting there:
Costs can vary depending on your starting point and mode of transportation. Approximate costs:
- Train from Bucharest: €15-€25

- Bus from Bucharest: €12-€20
- Car rental per day: €20-€40
- Flight to Sibiu + bus/train to Alba Iulia: €70-€150 (depending on origin)

Features and exploring the town:

1. Alba Carolina Citadel: The star attraction, this 18th-century fortress is beautifully restored and houses museums, cafes, and historical reenactments.

2. National Museum of Unification: Located in the citadel, it showcases the city's role in Romanian unification.

3. St. Michael's Roman Catholic Cathedral: The oldest and most valuable architectural monument in the city.

4. Batthyaneum Library: A historic library with a rich collection of rare books and manuscripts.

5. Third Gate of the Alba Carolina Citadel: Features an impressive Baroque sculptural group.

6. Reconciliation Park: A modern sculpture park symbolizing interethnic harmony.

7. Orthodox Cathedral of the Reunification: Built to commemorate the 1918 unification.

8. Roman Catholic Bishop's Palace: An impressive Baroque building in the citadel.

Tips for exploring:
- The main attractions are concentrated in and around the Alba Carolina Citadel, which is easily walkable.
- Join the free guided tours of the citadel offered by local volunteers.
- Watch the Guard Changing Ceremony in the citadel (usually held on weekends).
- Use the city's bike-sharing system to explore beyond the citadel.
- Visit during the Alba Iulia Music & Film Festival (usually in September) for cultural events.

Alba Iulia offers a unique blend of history, architecture, and culture. Its well-preserved citadel and numerous museums provide insight into Transylvania's rich past, while its modern developments offer contemporary comforts. The city is less crowded than some other Transylvanian destinations, allowing for a more relaxed exploration of its historical treasures.

CHAPTER 4. Must-See Attractions

Bran Castle (Dracula's Castle)

Bran Castle, often referred to as "Dracula's Castle," is one of the most famous attractions in Transylvania. Here are the key details about this iconic landmark:

Location:
Bran Castle is situated in the village of Bran, near Brașov, in central Romania. It stands on the border between Transylvania and Wallachia.

Historical Significance:
- Built in the 14th century, originally as a fortress to defend against the Ottoman Empire.

- Associated with Vlad the Impaler, the historical figure who inspired Bram Stoker's Dracula character.
- Despite popular belief, there's little historical evidence that Vlad ever owned or lived in the castle.

Architecture:
- The castle is a striking example of medieval architecture.
- Features tall towers, narrow winding staircases, and underground passages.
- Houses a collection of art and furniture collected by Queen Marie of Romania.

Dracula Connection:
- While the castle has no direct connection to the fictional Dracula, it matches Bram Stoker's description in his novel.
- The castle capitalizes on this association, featuring exhibits related to the Dracula legend.
Visitor Experience:
- Tours of the castle interior, including rooms decorated with period furniture.
- Exhibits on Romanian folklore, medieval customs, and the Dracula legend.
- Beautiful views of the surrounding Carpathian Mountains from the castle's balconies.

Practical Information:
- Open daily, with extended hours during peak tourist season.
- Admission fees are typically around 40-45 Romanian Lei (approx. €8-€9) for adults.
- Audio guides are available in multiple languages.
- The castle can get very crowded during peak season (summer months and around Halloween).

Nearby Attractions:
- The village of Bran offers souvenir shops, restaurants, and small museums.
- Hiking trails in the nearby Bucegi Mountains.

Getting There:
- Most visitors come from nearby Braşov, about 30 km away.
- Regular buses run from Braşov to Bran.
- Taxis and organized tours are also available.

Best Time to Visit:
- Spring and fall offer milder weather and fewer crowds.
- For a spooky atmosphere, consider visiting around Halloween when special events are often held.

While Bran Castle's connection to the real Dracula (Vlad the Impaler) is tenuous, it remains a must-see attraction for its historical value, stunning architecture, and the romantic allure of the Dracula legend. The castle offers a fascinating glimpse into Transylvanian history and medieval life, set against the backdrop of the beautiful Carpathian landscape.

Peleş Castle

Peleş Castle is indeed one of the must-see attractions in Romania, although it's technically just outside Transylvania in the neighboring region of Wallachia. Here are the details about this stunning castle:

Location:
Peleş Castle is situated in Sinaia, a mountain resort town in Prahova County, about 124 km north of Bucharest and 48 km south of Braşov. It's nestled in the Carpathian Mountains, surrounded by beautiful forests.

History:
- Built between 1873 and 1914 for King Carol I of Romania
- Served as the summer residence of the Romanian royal family until 1947
- Became a museum in 1953

Architecture and Style:
- Neo-Renaissance architecture with elements of German and Italian styles
- Considered one of the most stunning castles in Europe
- Features over 160 rooms, each decorated in a different style

Notable Features:
1. Ornate wood carvings and stained glass windows
2. Extensive art collection including sculptures, paintings, and tapestries
3. One of the finest collections of arms and armor in Eastern Europe

4. A movie theater, one of the first in Europe
5. Advanced features for its time, including central heating and electricity

Visiting Information:
- Open: Tuesday to Sunday (closed on Mondays)
- Hours typically 9:15 AM to 5 PM (last admission at 4:15 PM), but can vary seasonally
- Guided tours are available in several languages
- Photography is allowed inside for an additional fee

Getting There:
- By train: Regular trains run from Bucharest to Sinaia
- By car: About a 1.5-hour drive from Bucharest
- Organized tours are available from Bucharest and nearby cities

Tips for Visitors:
- Book tickets in advance, especially during peak season
- Wear comfortable shoes as there's a bit of a climb to reach the castle
- Consider combining your visit with nearby Pelişor Castle
- The castle can be crowded in summer; spring or fall visits might be more comfortable

Peleş Castle offers a glimpse into the luxurious life of Romanian royalty and is renowned for its architectural beauty and historical significance. Its picturesque setting and lavish interiors make it a favorite among tourists visiting Romania.

Corvin Castle

Corvin Castle, also known as Hunyad Castle or Hunedoara Castle, is one of the largest castles in Europe and arguably the most stunning medieval castle in Romania. Here are the key details:

Location:
The castle is located in Hunedoara, a city in southwestern Transylvania, Romania.

Historical Significance:
- Built in the 15th century on the site of an older fortification
- Associated with John Hunyadi, a leading Hungarian military and political figure
- Later expanded and renovated in Renaissance and Gothic styles

Architecture:
- A blend of Gothic and Renaissance architectural styles
- Features tall towers, bastions, an inner courtyard, and a drawbridge
- Notable for its large and imposing structure with over 50 rooms

Key Features:
1. Knights' Hall: A large room used for feasts and ceremonies
2. Diet Hall: Where the Transylvanian Diet (assembly) would meet
3. Bear Pit: A deep well where bears were once kept
4. Capistrano Tower: Named after a Franciscan monk, offers panoramic views
5. Neboise Tower: The castle's torture chamber
6. The Chapel: Small but beautifully decorated
7. The Legend of the Ravens: Carved stone ravens adorn the walls, tied to a local legend

Visiting Information:
- Open year-round, but hours may vary seasonally
- Guided tours available in multiple languages
- Allow 2-3 hours for a thorough visit

How to Get There:
- By car: About 1.5 hours from Sibiu or 4 hours from Bucharest
- By train: To Hunedoara station, then a short taxi ride
- By bus: Services available from major cities in Romania

Historical Legends:
- Said to be where Vlad the Impaler (the inspiration for Dracula) was held prisoner
- Various ghost stories and legends associated with the castle

Cultural Impact:
- Featured in several movies and TV shows
- Inspiration for Castle Dracula in Bram Stoker's novel (though Bran Castle is more commonly associated with this)

Preservation:
The castle has undergone several restoration projects to maintain its structure and historical integrity, making it one of the best-preserved medieval castles in Europe.

Corvin Castle offers visitors a chance to step back in time and experience the grandeur of medieval Transylvania. Its impressive architecture, rich history, and atmospheric setting make it a highlight of any trip to Romania.

Transfăgărășan Highway

The Transfăgărășan Highway is indeed one of Romania's must-see attractions. Here are the details about this remarkable road:

Description:
The Transfăgărășan (pronounced tran-sfuh-guh-ruh-shahn) is a paved mountain road crossing the southern section of the Carpathian Mountains. It's often described as one of the most spectacular roads in the world, known for its sharp hairpin turns, long S-curves, and dramatic ascents and descents.

Location:
The road connects the historic regions of Transylvania and Wallachia, crossing the Făgăraș Mountains, which are part of the Carpathians. It runs between the cities of Sibiu in the north and Pitești in the south.

Length and Elevation:
- Total length: About 90 kilometers (56 miles)
- Highest point: 2,042 meters (6,699 feet) at Bâlea Lake

Key Features:
1. Bâlea Lake: A glacier lake at the road's highest point, with a chalet and cable car.
2. Bâlea Waterfall: A stunning 60-meter high waterfall accessible by cable car.
3. Vidraru Dam: A hydroelectric dam on the Argeș River, offering beautiful views.
4. Poenari Castle: A ruined castle associated with Vlad the Impaler, accessible via 1,480 steps.

Best Time to Visit:
The road is typically open from late June to late October, depending on weather conditions. July and August are the peak months, offering the best weather but also the most traffic.

Driving Experience:
- The road is challenging, with steep inclines and sharp turns.
- Speed limit is generally 40 km/h (25 mph).
- The journey can take 3-4 hours without stops, but most travelers take a full day to enjoy the scenery.

Tips for Visitors:
1. Check road conditions before traveling, as weather can change quickly.
2. Start early to avoid crowds and have more time for stops.
3. Ensure your vehicle is in good condition, especially the brakes.
4. Bring warm clothing, even in summer, as temperatures can be much cooler at higher elevations.
5. Consider renting a car in Sibiu or Bucharest if you're not driving your own vehicle.

Historical Note:
The road was built between 1970 and 1974 during Nicolae Ceauşescu's regime, primarily as a strategic military route.

Cultural Impact:
The Transfăgărăşan gained international fame after being featured on the British TV show "Top Gear," where it was called "the best road in the world."

The Transfăgărăşan Highway offers not just a means of transportation, but an unforgettable journey through some of Romania's most breathtaking landscapes. It's a must-see for road trip enthusiasts, nature lovers, and anyone looking to experience the raw beauty of the Carpathian Mountains.

Turda Salt Mine

Turda Salt Mine is indeed one of the must-see attractions in Transylvania. Here are the details about this unique site:

Location:
Turda Salt Mine is located in Turda, a city in Cluj County, Romania. It's about 30 km southeast of Cluj-Napoca, the largest city in Transylvania.

History:
- The mine dates back to the Middle Ages, with salt extraction beginning as early as 1075.
- It was actively used for salt extraction until 1932.

- After closure, it was used as a cheese storage facility and later as a bomb shelter during World War II.
- In 1992, it was reopened as a tourist attraction and underwent significant renovations.

Features:

1. Rudolf Mine: The largest chamber, featuring a 50-meter tall extraction bell.

2. Underground Lake: A 8-meter deep salt lake where visitors can rent rowboats.

3. Ferris Wheel: A 20-meter tall wheel offering unique views of the mine.

4. Amphitheater: Used for concerts and events due to its excellent acoustics.

5. Salt Museum: Displays tools and machines used in salt mining.

6. Treatment Rooms: Areas where visitors can experience salt therapy.

7. Sports Facilities: Including mini-golf, table tennis, and bowling alleys.

8. Elevator: A modern addition for easier access to different levels.

Visitor Information:

- Opening Hours: Usually open daily, but hours may vary by season.
- Admission: Prices are typically around 40-50 RON (€8-€10) for adults, with discounts for children and seniors.
- Temperature: Constant 10-12°C (50-54°F) year-round, so bring warm clothing.
- Accessibility: While there's an elevator, some areas require walking on uneven surfaces.
- Guided Tours: Available in multiple languages, often need to be booked in advance.

How to Get There:
- From Cluj-Napoca: Regular bus services or a 30-40 minute drive.
- From other parts of Transylvania: Accessible by car or organized tours.

Tips for Visitors:
- Allow at least 2-3 hours for your visit.
- Wear comfortable, non-slip shoes.
- Bring a camera - the lighting and structures make for stunning photos.
- Consider visiting during weekdays to avoid crowds.
- If you have respiratory issues, the salt-rich air might be beneficial, but consult your doctor first.

Turda Salt Mine offers a unique blend of history, natural wonder, and modern entertainment facilities. Its transformation from an industrial site to a futuristic attraction makes it a standout destination in Transylvania.

CHAPTER 5. Natural Wonders and Outdoor Activities

Carpathian Mountains

The Carpathian Mountains are a significant natural feature of Transylvania and Romania as a whole. Here are details about this mountain range:

Location:
The Carpathians form a 1,500 km-long mountain range in Central and Eastern Europe. They extend through several countries, with a large portion in Romania, including Transylvania.

Geographical features:
- Highest peak in Romania: Moldoveanu Peak (2,544 m)
- Diverse landscapes: Dense forests, alpine meadows, rocky peaks, and glacial lakes
- Rich biodiversity: Home to various flora and fauna, including large populations of brown bears, wolves, and lynx

Outdoor activities:

1. Hiking: Numerous trails for all skill levels
   - Popular routes: Fagaras Mountains, Retezat National Park, Piatra Craiului National Park

2. Skiing and winter sports:
   - Major resorts: Poiana Brasov, Sinaia, Predeal

3. Rock climbing: Many locations for both beginners and experienced climbers
   - Notable areas: Bicaz Gorges, Piatra Craiului

4. Mountain biking: Extensive network of trails
   - Example: Postavarul Massif near Brasov

5. Wildlife watching: Guided tours to observe bears, birds, and other wildlife

6. Caving: Explored and unexplored cave systems
   - Notable cave: Scarisoara Ice Cave

7. Rafting and kayaking: On rivers like the Jiu, Buzau, and Crisul Repede

8. Camping: Many designated campsites throughout the mountains

Conservation:
The Carpathians are home to several national parks and protected areas, including:
- Retezat National Park
- Piatra Craiului National Park
- Calimani National Park

Cultural significance:
- Traditional rural life: Many villages in the Carpathians maintain traditional ways of life
- Folklore: Rich in legends and myths, often featuring the mountains
- Historical sites: Ancient Dacian fortresses, medieval castles, and old churches dot the landscape

Best time to visit:
- Summer (June-August): Ideal for hiking and most outdoor activities
- Winter (December-February): Best for skiing and winter sports
- Spring/Autumn: Good for hiking with fewer crowds, beautiful scenery

Accessibility:
- Major cities near the Carpathians (e.g., Brasov, Sibiu) have airports and train connections
- Many mountain areas are accessible by car, though some remote locations may require 4x4 vehicles
- Guided tours are available for various activities and locations

The Carpathian Mountains offer a wealth of natural beauty and outdoor activities, making them a major attraction for visitors to Transylvania. Their diverse ecosystems, rich wildlife, and cultural heritage provide opportunities for both adventure and cultural exploration.

Retezat National Park

Retezat National Park is one of Romania's most beautiful and biodiverse protected areas. Here are the details about this natural wonder:

Location:
Retezat National Park is situated in the southwestern part of Transylvania, in the Southern Carpathians (also known as the Transylvanian Alps). It's located in Hunedoara County, Romania.

Size and Establishment:
- Area: Approximately 38,000 hectares (380 km²)

- Established: 1935, making it Romania's first national park

Geographical Features:
- Mountain peaks: Over 20 peaks above 2,000 meters
- Highest peak: Peleaga Peak (2,509 meters)
- Glacial lakes: Over 80 permanent glacial lakes, including the largest glacial lake in Romania, Bucura Lake
- Forests: Extensive areas of old-growth forests

Biodiversity:
- Flora: Over 1,190 plant species, including rare and endemic species
- Fauna: Rich wildlife including chamois, red deer, roe deer, wild boar, brown bears, wolves, and lynx
- Birds: Over 185 bird species recorded

Outdoor Activities:

1. Hiking:
   - Numerous marked trails of varying difficulty
   - Popular routes include trails to Bucura Lake and Peleaga Peak

2. Camping:
   - Several designated camping areas within the park

3. Wildlife watching:
   - Guided tours available for wildlife observation

4. Photography:
   - Stunning landscapes and diverse wildlife offer excellent photography opportunities
5. Mountain climbing:
   - Several peaks suitable for experienced climbers

6. Fishing:
- Permitted in certain areas with appropriate licenses

Best Time to Visit:
- Summer (June-August): Ideal for hiking and most outdoor activities
- Spring (May-June): Beautiful wildflowers bloom
- Autumn (September-October): Spectacular fall colors

Access and Accommodation:
- Nearest towns: Hateg and Lupeni
- Access points: Main entrances at Nucsoara and Carnic
- Accommodation: Mountain huts within the park, hotels and guesthouses in nearby towns

Regulations:
- Entrance fee required
- Strict regulations to protect the ecosystem (e.g., no off-trail hiking, no campfires outside designated areas)

Unique Features:
- Retezat is part of the UNESCO Man and Biosphere Programme
- It's one of the last remaining areas in Europe with pristine mixed forests and intact ecosystems
- The park contains some of the wildest and least-explored areas in the Carpathians

Guided Tours:
- Available from local tour operators, offering experiences ranging from day hikes to multi-day trekking expeditions
Retezat National Park offers a unique opportunity to experience some of Romania's most pristine wilderness. Its diverse landscapes, from glacial lakes to alpine meadows and

dense forests, provide a haven for wildlife and a paradise for nature enthusiasts. The park's strict conservation measures help preserve its natural beauty and ecological importance.

Apuseni Nature Park

Apuseni Nature Park is a stunning natural area in the Western Carpathians, partially located in Transylvania. Here are the details:

Location:
- Situated in the Apuseni Mountains, part of the Western Carpathians
- Spans three counties: Alba, Bihor, and Cluj
- Covers an area of approximately 75,784 hectares

Geographical features:
- Karst landscape with numerous caves, sinkholes, and underground rivers
- Forests, meadows, and alpine areas
- Elevation ranging from 300 to 1,849 meters (Curcubăta Mare peak)

Key attractions:

1. Caves:
    - Scărişoara Ice Cave: Houses one of the largest underground glaciers in Europe
    - Bears' Cave: Known for its bear fossils and impressive stalactites and stalagmites
    - Vârtop Cave: Contains human footprints dating back 62,000 years

2. Waterfalls:
 - Vârciorog Waterfall
 - Bohodei Waterfall

3. Gorges:
 - Galbenei Gorges
 - Sighiștelului Gorges

4. Lakes:
 - Warm Lake of Garda (Lacul Cald)
 - Bălileasa Lake

Outdoor activities:

1. Hiking: Extensive network of marked trails
2. Caving: Both guided tours and speleology expeditions
3. Rock climbing: Several established routes
4. Mountain biking: Trails of varying difficulty
5. Skiing: Small resorts like Vârtop and Arieșeni
6. Wildlife watching: Opportunities to observe diverse flora and fauna
7. Photography: Stunning landscapes and natural features

Biodiversity:
 - Rich flora: Over 1,550 plant species, including rare and endemic plants
 - Diverse fauna: Brown bears, wolves, lynx, and various bird species

Cultural aspects:
 - Traditional villages with unique architecture
 - Local crafts like woodcarving and textile weaving
 - Folk festivals and events throughout the year

Best time to visit:
- Spring to autumn for most outdoor activities
- Winter for skiing and winter sports

Accessibility:
- Nearest major cities: Cluj-Napoca, Oradea
- Accessible by car, though some areas require 4x4 vehicles
- Limited public transportation; private transfers or guided tours recommended

Accommodation:
- Mountain lodges and chalets within the park
- Guesthouses in nearby villages
- Camping sites for those who prefer outdoor stays

Conservation efforts:
- Protected area status helps preserve unique karst formations and biodiversity
- Sustainable tourism initiatives to balance visitor access with environmental protection

Visitor centers:
- Main center in Sudrigiu village, offering information and educational programs

Apuseni Nature Park offers a unique blend of natural wonders, outdoor adventures, and cultural experiences. Its karst landscape, rich biodiversity, and traditional rural life make it a distinctive destination within Transylvania, appealing to nature lovers, adventure seekers, and those interested in local culture.

Hiking and Trekking Routes

Hiking and trekking are popular activities in Transylvania, offering a range of routes through diverse landscapes. Here are details about some notable hiking and trekking routes:

1. Fagaras Mountains
   - Location: Southern Carpathians
   - Difficulty: Moderate to challenging
   - Notable route: Fagaras Ridge Trail
     - Length: About 70-90 km
     - Duration: 5-7 days
       - Highlights: Highest peaks in Romania, including Moldoveanu Peak (2,544m)

2. Piatra Craiului National Park
   - Location: Southern Carpathians, near Brasov

- Difficulty: Moderate to difficult
- Notable route: The Main Ridge Trail
  - Length: About 25 km
  - Duration: 1-2 days
  - Highlights: Limestone ridge, diverse flora and fauna

3. Retezat National Park
  - Location: Southern Carpathians
  - Difficulty: Easy to challenging
  - Notable route: Bucura Lake Circuit
  - Length: About 20 km
  - Duration: 1-2 days
  - Highlights: Glacial lakes, diverse landscapes

4. Apuseni Natural Park
  - Location: Western Carpathians
  - Difficulty: Easy to moderate
  - Notable route: Padis Plateau Circuit
  - Length: About 30 km
  - Duration: 2-3 days
  - Highlights: Karst formations, caves, waterfalls

5. Calimani National Park
  - Location: Eastern Carpathians
  - Difficulty: Moderate
  - Notable route: 12 Apostles Trail
  - Length: About 15 km
  - Duration: 1 day
  - Highlights: Volcanic landscapes, unique rock formations

6. Bicaz Gorges-Hasmas National Park
  - Location: Eastern Carpathians
  - Difficulty: Easy to moderate
  - Notable route: Bicaz Gorges Trail

- Length: About 8 km
- Duration: 3-4 hours
- Highlights: Dramatic limestone cliffs, Red Lake

7. Cozia National Park
  - Location: Southern Carpathians
  - Difficulty: Moderate
  - Notable route: Cozia Peak Trail
  - Length: About 16 km round trip
  - Duration: 1 day
  - Highlights: Panoramic views, diverse flora

General tips for hiking in Transylvania:
- Best season: Late spring to early autumn (May to September)
- Accommodation: Mountain huts (cabanas) available on many routes
- Safety: Inform others of your plans, carry proper equipment
- Guides: Available for hire, especially recommended for challenging routes
- Maps: Detailed hiking maps available for most areas
- Wildlife: Be aware of potential encounters with bears and other wildlife

Before embarking on any hike, especially multi-day treks, it's crucial to:
- Check current trail conditions
- Ensure you have appropriate gear and supplies
- Be aware of weather forecasts
- Register with mountain rescue services for longer, more remote treks

These routes offer a range of experiences, from easy day hikes to challenging multi-day treks, allowing hikers to explore Transylvania's natural beauty at various levels of difficulty.

Winter Sports and Ski Resorts

Winter sports and ski resorts are popular attractions in Transylvania, particularly in the Carpathian Mountains. Here are details about winter sports and notable ski resorts in the region:

Popular Winter Sports:
1. Skiing (downhill and cross-country)
2. Snowboarding
3. Ice skating
4. Sledding
5. Snowshoeing
6. Ice climbing (for advanced enthusiasts)

Notable Ski Resorts:

1. Poiana Brasov
   Location: Near Brasov city, about 170 km north of Bucharest
   Features:
   - Largest ski resort in Romania
   - 12 slopes with a total length of 25 km
   - Modern ski lifts and cable cars
   - Suitable for beginners to advanced skiers
   - Night skiing available
   - Ski school and equipment rental
   Nearby attractions: Brasov's medieval old town, Bran Castle

2. Sinaia
   Location: About 125 km north of Bucharest

Features:
- 20 km of slopes
- Varied terrain suitable for all levels
- Gondola and chair lifts
- Snowmaking capabilities
- Beautiful mountain scenery
Nearby attractions: Peles Castle, Sinaia Monastery

3. Predeal
Location: About 150 km north of Bucharest
Features:
- Highest town in Romania (1,030 m altitude)
- 8 slopes of varying difficulty
- Suitable for beginners and intermediate skiers
- Ski school and equipment rental
Nearby attractions: Peles Castle, Rasnov Fortress

4. Straja
Location: In Hunedoara County, western Transylvania
Features:
- 12 slopes with a total length of 26 km
- Modern ski lifts
- Suitable for all skill levels
- Snowmaking facilities
Nearby attractions: Corvin Castle in Hunedoara

5. Paltinis
Location: Near Sibiu, southern Transylvania
Features:
- Oldest ski resort in Romania
- 4 slopes of varying difficulty
- Cross-country skiing trails
- Ski school and equipment rental

Nearby attractions: Sibiu's old town, ASTRA National Museum Complex

Season and Conditions:
- The ski season typically runs from December to April, depending on snow conditions
- Best snow conditions are usually from January to March
- Many resorts have snowmaking capabilities to extend the season

Additional Information:
- Prices: Generally more affordable compared to Western European resorts
- Accommodations: Range from budget hostels to luxury hotels
- Apres-ski: Varies by resort, but generally includes restaurants, bars, and some nightlife
- Other activities: Many resorts offer additional winter activities like tubing, snowmobiling, and ice skating

Transportation:
- Most resorts are accessible by car or bus from major cities
- Some resorts offer shuttle services from nearby towns or airports

Tips:
- Book in advance for peak periods (Christmas, New Year, school holidays)
- Check snow reports and resort websites for current conditions
- Consider purchasing travel insurance that covers winter sports

Winter sports in Transylvania offer a mix of modern facilities and beautiful natural settings, often at more affordable prices than many Western European destinations. The proximity to historical and cultural attractions adds to the appeal, allowing visitors to combine winter sports with cultural exploration.

CHAPTER 6. Cultural Experiences

Traditional Villages and Rural Tourism

Traditional villages and rural tourism in Transylvania offer a unique cultural experience. Here's information on some notable areas:

1. Viscri Village

Location: Brasov County, central Romania

How to get there:
- By car: About 1 hour from Sighisoara or 2 hours from Brasov
- Public transport: Limited. Best to hire a car or join a tour

Cost of getting there:
- Car rental: €20-40 per day
- Organized tour from Brasov: €50-100 per person

Features:
- UNESCO World Heritage site
- 12th-century fortified church
- Traditional Saxon architecture
- Prince Charles owns a property here

Exploring/Cost:
- Walking tour of the village: Free or €10-20 with a guide
- Horse-cart rides: €15-30 per hour
- Accommodation in traditional houses: €30-70 per night

2. Maramures Region

Location: Northern Transylvania

How to get there:
- Fly to Cluj-Napoca or Baia Mare, then rent a car
- Train to Baia Mare, then local buses or car rental

Cost of getting there:
- Flights to Cluj-Napoca: €50-200 from European cities
- Car rental: €20-40 per day

Features:
- Wooden churches (UNESCO World Heritage sites)
- Traditional crafts: woodcarving, weaving
- Merry Cemetery in Sapanta
- Steam train: Mocanita on Vaser Valley

Exploring/Cost:
- Guided tour of the region: €50-100 per day
- Entry to wooden churches: €1-3 each
- Merry Cemetery entry: €3
- Mocanita steam train: €10-20

3. Sibiel

Location: Near Sibiu, southern Transylvania

How to get there:
- 20-minute drive from Sibiu
- Public bus from Sibiu (infrequent service)

Cost of getting there:
- Bus fare: €1-2 one way
- Taxi from Sibiu: €10-15

Features:
- Traditional Transylvanian village

- Museum of painted glass icons
- Home-stay experiences

Exploring/Cost:
- Museum entry: €2-3
- Home-cooked meal with locals: €15-25
- Accommodation in local guesthouses: €25-50 per night

4. Biertan

Location: Sibiu County, central Romania

How to get there:
- 30-minute drive from Sighisoara
- Limited public transport; car rental recommended

Cost of getting there:
- Car rental: €20-40 per day

Features:
- UNESCO World Heritage fortified church
- Well-preserved medieval architecture
- Annual truffle festival

Exploring/Cost:
- Church entry: €2-3
- Guided tour of the village: €10-20
- Truffle hunting experience (seasonal): €50-100

General Tips for Rural Tourism in Transylvania:

1. Language: English is not widely spoken in rural areas. Consider hiring a guide or learning basic Romanian phrases.

2. Accommodation: Many villages offer "casa de oaspeti" (guesthouses) for an authentic experience.

3. Food: Try local specialties like "sarmale" (stuffed cabbage rolls) and "cozonac" (sweet bread).

4. Respect local customs: Many rural areas are traditional; dress modestly when visiting churches.

5. Transportation: While public transport exists, it's often limited. Renting a car provides the most flexibility for exploring rural areas.

6. Timing: Spring and early fall offer pleasant weather and the chance to witness traditional agricultural activities.

7. Crafts: Many villages specialize in particular crafts. Look for opportunities to watch artisans at work or participate in workshops.

Rural tourism in Transylvania offers an immersive cultural experience, allowing visitors to step back in time and experience traditional Romanian life. Costs are generally lower than in urban areas, making it an affordable way to explore the region's rich heritage.

Folk Festivals and Events

Transylvania is rich in cultural traditions and hosts numerous folk festivals and events throughout the year. Here are some notable ones:

1. Sighișoara Medieval Festival
   - Location: Sighișoara

- Timing: Usually late July
- Description: A three-day festival celebrating medieval arts, crafts, and culture. Features costumed parades, knight tournaments, traditional music and dance performances.

2. Târgu Mureş Days
  - Location: Târgu Mureş
  - Timing: Late June
  - Description: A week-long celebration of local culture with concerts, art exhibitions, and traditional food fairs.

3. Transylvanian International Film Festival (TIFF)
  - Location: Cluj-Napoca
  - Timing: Late May to early June
  - Description: Romania's largest film festival, showcasing international and Romanian films.

4. Sibiu International Theatre Festival
  - Location: Sibiu
  - Timing: June
  - Description: One of the largest performing arts festivals in the world, featuring theatre, dance, and music performances.

5. Pentecost Pilgrimage (Csíksomlyó Pilgrimage)
  - Location: Şumuleu Ciuc (Csíksomlyó)
  - Timing: Pentecost weekend (usually in May or June)
  - Description: A major Hungarian Catholic pilgrimage and celebration of Szekler culture.

6. Sânziene Festival (Midsummer Day)
  - Location: Various locations across Transylvania
  - Timing: June 24
  - Description: A traditional festival celebrating the summer solstice with bonfires, floral wreaths, and folk rituals.

7. Hora de la Prislop
   - Location: Prislop Pass
   - Timing: August
   - Description: A traditional folk festival featuring music, dance, and customs from various regions of Transylvania.

8. Oktoberfest Brasov
   - Location: Brașov
   - Timing: September
   - Description: A celebration of German culture and beer, reflecting the region's Saxon heritage.

9. Festivalul Verzei (Cabbage Festival)
   - Location: Mosna
   - Timing: October
   - Description: A quirky festival celebrating the humble cabbage, with traditional dishes and cultural events.

10. Transylvanian Christmas Markets
    - Location: Various cities (notably Sibiu, Brașov, Cluj-Napoca)
    - Timing: December
    - Description: Traditional Christmas markets featuring local crafts, food, and festive atmosphere.

These festivals and events offer visitors a chance to experience Transylvanian culture firsthand, from medieval reenactments to contemporary arts. They showcase the region's diverse heritage, including Romanian, Hungarian, German, and Roma influences.

When planning to attend any of these events, it's advisable to:
- Check current dates, as they can vary slightly from year to year

- Book accommodation in advance, as popular events can attract large crowds
- Research any specific customs or dress codes associated with traditional events
- Consider guided tours that might offer deeper insights into the cultural significance of these festivals

Museums and Art Galleries

Here's a narrative that covers several key cultural institutions:

My journey through Transylvania's museums and art galleries was a fascinating dive into the region's rich history and vibrant artistic scene. I'll share my experiences at some of the most memorable locations.

1. Brukenthal National Museum, Sibiu

My first stop was the Brukenthal National Museum in Sibiu. Located in the heart of the city's historic center on Piața Mare (Large Square), it was easy to find. I walked there from my hotel, but there are also local buses if you're staying further out.

The museum is housed in a stunning Baroque palace, and the entrance fee was about 20 lei (roughly 4 EUR). Inside, I was amazed by the extensive European art collection, including works by Flemish, Dutch, and German masters. The museum also houses impressive archaeological artifacts and a vast library.

What struck me most was the juxtaposition of this grand, European-style museum against the backdrop of a Transylvanian city. Don't miss the room dedicated to Transylvanian art - it provides a unique local perspective.

2. ASTRA National Museum Complex, Sibiu

Just a short taxi ride from Sibiu's center (about 15 lei or 3 EUR), I found myself at the ASTRA National Museum Complex. The entrance fee was around 30 lei (6 EUR), which I found very reasonable given the museum's size.

This open-air museum was unlike anything I'd seen before. Spread across a vast park, it features over 300 buildings representing traditional Romanian village life. I spent hours wandering through reconstructed homes, workshops, and churches, each telling a story of Romania's rural past.

I'd recommend renting a bike at the entrance to cover more ground. Also, try to catch one of the craft demonstrations - I watched a fascinating presentation on traditional wool processing.

3. Corvinus Castle, Hunedoara

While not strictly a museum, this Gothic-Renaissance castle houses several exhibition spaces that make it a must-visit. It's

81

about a 2-hour drive from Sibiu, or you can take a train to Deva and then a local bus to Hunedoara.

The entrance fee was 35 lei (7 EUR), and it was worth every penny. The castle's architecture is stunning, with towering turrets and a drawbridge straight out of a fairy tale. Inside, I explored exhibits on medieval weaponry, period furniture, and the castle's history.

The torture room exhibition was particularly chilling. For a special treat, I timed my visit to coincide with one of their medieval festivals, complete with costumed reenactors and traditional music.

4. Székely National Museum, Sfântu Gheorghe

My next stop took me to the eastern part of Transylvania. I took a train from Braşov to Sfântu Gheorghe (about 1 hour, 15 lei or 3 EUR). The museum, dedicated to the culture of the Székely people, an ethnic Hungarian group in Romania, was a short walk from the station.

The entrance fee was modest at 15 lei (3 EUR). Inside, I found a treasure trove of ethnographic exhibits, including traditional costumes, crafts, and historical artifacts. The natural history section, with its extensive collection of Carpathian wildlife specimens, was particularly impressive.

What I enjoyed most was how this museum offered insight into a distinct cultural group within Transylvania, adding another layer to my understanding of the region's complex history.

5. Art Museum of Cluj-Napoca

My final stop was in Cluj-Napoca, Transylvania's largest city. The Art Museum is located in the beautiful Bánffy Palace in the city center, easily reachable on foot or by local bus from most parts of the city.

The entrance fee was 20 lei (4 EUR). The museum houses an excellent collection of Romanian art from the 15th to 20th centuries. I was particularly drawn to the works of Nicolae Grigorescu and Ion Andreescu, considered founders of modern Romanian painting.

What I found unique about this museum was its commitment to contemporary art. There was a thought-provoking temporary exhibition of local artists that really helped me understand the current cultural pulse of Transylvania.

Throughout my museum tour of Transylvania, I was continually surprised by the depth and diversity of the region's cultural offerings. From grand European art collections to intimate ethnographic displays, each museum added a new dimension to my understanding of this fascinating region. I'd highly recommend setting aside ample time to explore these cultural treasures - they're an essential part of any visit to Transylvania.

Thermal Spas and Wellness Centers

During my recent trip to Transylvania, I discovered a hidden gem of relaxation and rejuvenation - its thermal spas and wellness centers. Let me share my experiences with you.

My first stop was Băile Felix, one of Romania's most famous spa resorts. Located about 8 km from Oradea in northwestern Transylvania, I easily reached it by taking a 20-minute taxi ride from Oradea (costing around 50 RON or €10). The resort is renowned for its thermal waters rich in oligominerala.

At Băile Felix, I indulged in various treatments at the Apollo-Felix complex. A day pass cost me about 100 RON (€20), which included access to indoor and outdoor thermal pools, saunas, and relaxation areas. I particularly enjoyed the mud wraps, which are said to have therapeutic properties for joint issues.

Next, I ventured to Sovata, a picturesque town in the heart of Transylvania. I took a train from Cluj-Napoca to Târgu Mureş (about 2.5 hours, €10-15), then a local bus to Sovata (1 hour, €5). The town is famous for its salt lakes, especially Lake Ursu.

At Ensana Sovata Health Spa Hotel, I experienced their salt therapy treatments. A day pass was pricier at around 200 RON (€40), but it was worth it for access to their extensive facilities, including the unique salt cave. The floating experience in the salt lake was incredibly relaxing and reportedly good for skin conditions.

My final stop was Băile Tuşnad, the smallest town in Romania, nestled in the Eastern Carpathians. I reached it by train from Braşov (about 2 hours, €8-10). This quaint spa town is known for its carbonated mineral waters and mofette therapy - natural carbon dioxide emissions used for treating cardiovascular diseases.

At the Tusnad Wellness Center, I tried their carbonated mineral baths. A full day of spa access and treatments cost around 150 RON (€30). The center also offers excellent massage therapies, which I found perfect after days of traveling.

Throughout my spa journey, I noticed a few common features:
1. Most spas offer both day passes and individual treatment options.
2. Many have both indoor and outdoor facilities, making them year-round destinations.
3. Traditional treatments are often combined with modern wellness approaches.
4. Some spas have medical staff on hand for more specialized treatments.

A few tips for fellow travelers:
- Book treatments in advance, especially in peak season (June-August).
- Bring your own towel and flip-flops to save on rental costs.
- Many spas offer package deals for multiple days, which can be more economical.
- Don't hesitate to ask staff about the best treatments for your specific needs.

Cost implications varied, but generally:
- Day passes: 100-200 RON (€20-40)
- Individual treatments: 50-150 RON (€10-30) each
- Accommodation near spas: 200-500 RON (€40-100) per night, depending on luxury level

Overall, exploring Transylvania's thermal spas and wellness centers was a highlight of my trip. The combination of natural healing properties, beautiful surroundings, and affordable prices made it a truly rejuvenating experience. Whether you're looking to soothe sore muscles after hiking the Carpathians or simply want to relax, Transylvania's spa scene has something for everyone.

CHAPTER 7. Culinary Journey

Traditional Transylvanian Cuisine

As someone who's had the pleasure of exploring Transylvania's culinary landscape, I'd be delighted to share my experiences with traditional Transylvanian cuisine. The region's food is a delightful mix of Romanian, Hungarian, and Saxon influences, resulting in hearty, flavorful dishes that reflect the area's rich history and agricultural abundance.

Here are some standout dishes I encountered:

1. Mici (Mititei):
These are small, grilled meat rolls made from a mix of beef, lamb, and pork, seasoned with garlic and spices. I found them at almost every outdoor market and restaurant. They're typically served with mustard and bread. A portion of 3-5 mici usually costs around 15-25 RON (€3-5).

2. Sarmale:
Cabbage rolls stuffed with minced meat, rice, and spices, often served with polenta and sour cream. I had a delicious version at a small family-run restaurant in Sibiu. A serving typically costs 25-35 RON (€5-7).

3. Ciorbă de Burtă:
A sour tripe soup that's surprisingly delicious. It's often served with sour cream and hot peppers. I tried this at a traditional restaurant in Cluj-Napoca for about 20 RON (€4).

4. Cozonac:
A sweet bread filled with nuts, cocoa, and sometimes raisins. It's especially popular during holidays. I bought one from a local bakery in Brașov for around 15 RON (€3).

5. Kürtőskalács (Chimney Cake):
A sweet, spiral-shaped pastry roasted over charcoal. I found these at street markets in most towns. One cake usually costs 10-15 RON (€2-3).

6. Tocăniță:
A hearty stew made with various meats and vegetables. I had a fantastic pork tocăniță in a rural guesthouse near Sighișoara. Main dish prices in such places usually range from 30-45 RON (€6-9).

7. Papanași:
These are fried dough dumplings filled with sweet cheese, topped with sour cream and fruit jam. I indulged in these at a popular restaurant in Brașov for about 25 RON (€5).

8. Zacuscă:
A vegetable spread made primarily from roasted eggplant and red peppers. I bought a jar at a local market to enjoy with bread. A jar typically costs 10-20 RON (€2-4).

When it comes to drinks, I couldn't miss trying:

1. Țuică: A strong plum brandy, often homemade. A shot in a restaurant usually costs 5-10 RON (€1-2).
2. Palincă: Similar to țuică but can be made from various fruits. Prices are similar.
3. Local wines: Transylvania has some excellent wines. A glass in a restaurant typically costs 15-25 RON (€3-5).

A few tips for fellow food enthusiasts:

1. Try to eat at local, family-run restaurants for the most authentic experience.
2. Don't be afraid to try the street food, especially at markets and festivals.
3. Many dishes are quite heavy, so pace yourself!
4. Vegetarian options can be limited in traditional restaurants, but larger cities have more variety.
5. In rural areas, many guesthouses offer home-cooked meals using local ingredients.

Overall, I found Transylvanian cuisine to be hearty, flavorful, and excellent value for money. A typical meal in a mid-range restaurant, including a main dish and a drink, usually cost me between 50-80 RON (€10-16). In more upscale establishments in city centers, prices could go up to 100-150 RON (€20-30) per person for a full meal.

Remember, part of the joy of experiencing Transylvanian cuisine is the warm hospitality that often accompanies it. Don't hesitate to ask locals for their favorite spots - you might discover some hidden culinary gems!

Wine Regions and Tastings

As someone who's explored Transylvania's wine regions, I'm excited to share my experiences with you. Transylvania may not be as famous for wine as some other European regions, but it offers a unique and delightful wine tasting adventure.

1. Târnave Wine Region

My journey began in the Târnave region, located in central Transylvania. I reached it by renting a car in Cluj-Napoca (about €30-40 per day) and driving about 2 hours south.

Notable wineries:
- Jidvei Winery: The crown jewel of the region. I paid 50 RON (€10) for a tour and tasting of their famous dry white wines made from Fetească Regală and Sauvignon Blanc grapes.
- Liliac Winery: A bit pricier at 80 RON (€16) for a tasting, but their premium wines were worth it.

The rolling hills covered in vineyards were breathtaking, especially in late summer when the grapes were ripening.

2. Recaş Wine Region

Next, I headed to Recaş, near Timişoara in western Romania. I took a train from Cluj-Napoca to Timişoara (about 4 hours, €20-25), then a short taxi ride to Recaş (30 minutes, around €15).

Cramele Recaş is the major player here. Their tasting room offers a variety of experiences, from a basic tasting (40 RON, €8) to more elaborate food and wine pairings (100-150 RON, €20-30). I was particularly impressed with their Fetească Neagră, a local red variety.

3. Dealu Mare Wine Region

While technically just outside Transylvania, Dealu Mare is easily accessible and worth the trip. I took a train from Braşov to Ploiești (about 2 hours, €10), then arranged a wine tour through my accommodation.

Highlights:
- SERVE Winery: Known for its Fetească Neagră and Pinot Noir. Tasting was around 60 RON (€12).
- Lacerta Winery: A bit more upscale, offering a tasting with local cheeses for 100 RON (€20).

The region's climate is perfect for red wines, and the landscape of gentle hills reminded me of Tuscany.

What to do:
- Join guided tours: Many wineries offer tours that explain the winemaking process.
- Taste local varieties: Don't miss trying Fetească Regală, Fetească Albă, and Fetească Neagră.
- Food pairings: Some wineries offer local cheese and charcuterie with tastings.
- Harvest activities: If you visit in September-October, you might participate in grape harvesting.

Cost implications:
- Winery tours and tastings: 40-150 RON (€8-30) depending on the winery and package.
- Accommodation: 200-400 RON (€40-80) per night in nearby towns.
- Transportation: Renting a car is often the most convenient option, costing about €30-40 per day.
- Guided wine tours: Full-day tours including transport and multiple wineries can cost 300-500 RON (€60-100) per person.

Tips:
1. Book tastings in advance, especially during peak season (May-October).
2. Consider hiring a driver or joining a tour if you plan to visit multiple wineries in a day.
3. Learn a few Romanian wine terms to enhance your experience.
4. Many wineries offer shipping services if you want to send some bottles home.

Transylvania's wine regions offer a less crowded, more intimate wine tasting experience compared to more famous European destinations. The combination of unique local grape varieties, beautiful landscapes, and warm Romanian hospitality made for an unforgettable journey through the flavors of Transylvania.

Best Restaurants and Cafes

As a traveler exploring Transylvania's culinary scene, I discovered some fantastic restaurants and cafes. Here's my experience with some of the best:

1. Crama Sibiul Vechi (Sibiu)
Location: Piața Mică 16, Sibiu
How to get there: Located in Sibiu's Small Square, it's easily walkable from anywhere in the old town.

This traditional Romanian restaurant is set in a 15th-century wine cellar. I tried their famous "Tochitura Sibiana" (a hearty meat stew) and "Sarmale" (stuffed cabbage rolls). The ambiance was incredible, with rustic decor and live folk music some evenings.

Dishes: Traditional Romanian cuisine
Cost: Main courses 40-80 RON (€8-16)

2. Bistro de l'Arte (Braşov)
Location: Piaţa George Enescu 11A, Braşov
How to get there: A short walk from Braşov's main square, Council Square.

This charming bistro offers a fusion of Romanian and international cuisine. I loved their "Transylvanian Goulash" and the creative desserts. The cozy, artsy atmosphere made it perfect for both lunch and dinner.

Dishes: Romanian fusion, international cuisine
Cost: Main courses 35-70 RON (€7-14)

3. Kürtőskalács Manufaktúra (Cluj-Napoca)
Location: Bulevardul Eroilor 21, Cluj-Napoca
How to get there: Centrally located on one of Cluj's main boulevards, easily reached on foot or by public transport.

This isn't a restaurant, but a must-visit cafe specializing in "Kürtőskalács" (chimney cake), a traditional Transylvanian sweet treat. I tried both classic and filled versions - the chocolate-filled was my favorite.

Dishes: Various flavors of Kürtőskalács
Cost: 10-20 RON (€2-4) per cake

4. La Ceaunu' Crapat (Sighişoara)
Location: Str. Bastionului 1, Sighişoara
How to get there: Inside the citadel walls of Sighişoara's old town, a short walk from the Clock Tower.

Set in a medieval house, this restaurant offers authentic Transylvanian cuisine. Their "Bulz" (polenta stuffed with cheese and bacon) was delicious, as was the "Cocoş de Munte" (mountain rooster stew).

Dishes: Traditional Transylvanian cuisine
Cost: Main courses 35-75 RON (€7-15)

5. Cafeneaua Verde (Braşov)
Location: Strada Mureşenilor 19, Braşov
How to get there: Just off the main pedestrian street in Braşov's old town.

This cozy cafe is perfect for breakfast or a light lunch. They offer great coffee, fresh juices, and delicious vegetarian options. I particularly enjoyed their avocado toast and smoothie bowls.

Dishes: International cafe fare, vegetarian options
Cost: Breakfast/light meals 20-40 RON (€4-8)

6. Containerul (Cluj-Napoca)
Location: Piaţa Unirii 31-32, Cluj-Napoca
How to get there: Right on the main square of Cluj-Napoca, impossible to miss.

This unique restaurant is built from shipping containers. They offer a modern take on Romanian cuisine. I tried their duck breast with forest fruit sauce and it was excellent. The cocktails here are also creative and delicious.

Dishes: Modern Romanian cuisine, international dishes
Cost: Main courses 45-90 RON (€9-18)

General tips:
- Reservations are recommended for dinner at popular restaurants, especially on weekends.
- Many restaurants offer a "daily menu" (meniu zilei) at lunchtime, which is usually great value.
- Tipping is customary in Romania, usually 10% for good service.
- Try the local wines - Romania has some excellent varieties that pair well with the cuisine.

Overall, I found Transylvanian restaurants to offer great value for money, with a wide range of options from traditional to modern cuisine. Don't be afraid to try local specialties - they're often the highlight of the menu!

Food Markets and Cooking Classes

As a food enthusiast exploring Transylvania, I discovered some fantastic food markets and cooking classes. Here's what I experienced:

Food Markets:

1. Piata Centrala (Central Market), Cluj-Napoca
Location: Piața Unirii, Cluj-Napoca
How to get there: Located in the city center, easily walkable from most parts of Cluj.
Items sold: Fresh produce, meats, cheeses, honey, traditional pastries
Cost: Varies, but generally very affordable. Examples:
- 1 kg of tomatoes: 5-10 RON (€1-2)
- Homemade cheese: 20-30 RON/kg (€4-6)
- Local honey: 25-40 RON/jar (€5-8)

2. Piața Obor, Brașov
Location: Strada Lungă 39, Brașov
How to get there: Take bus lines 4 or 41 from the city center.
Items sold: Organic produce, artisanal products, traditional Transylvanian foods
Cost: Slightly higher than supermarkets, but quality is excellent. Examples:
- Organic apples: 8-12 RON/kg (€1.6-2.4)
- Homemade jams: 15-25 RON/jar (€3-5)
- Traditional sausages: 40-60 RON/kg (€8-12)

3. Piața Cibin, Sibiu
Location: Piața Cibin, Sibiu
How to get there: A short walk from Sibiu's old town.
Items sold: Local produce, meats, dairy products, handicrafts
Cost: Very reasonable prices. Examples:
- Fresh eggs: 1 RON each (€0.2)
- Local cheese varieties: 25-35 RON/kg (€5-7)
- Homemade pickles: 10-15 RON/jar (€2-3)

Cooking Classes:

1. My Transylvania
Address: Strada Lungă 105, Brașov
Recipes taught: Traditional Transylvanian dishes like Sarmale (stuffed cabbage rolls), Cozonac (sweet bread), and Bulz (polenta with cheese)
Duration: 3-4 hours
Cost: Around 200-250 RON (€40-50) per person

2. Sibiu Cooking Class
Address: Piața Mică 16, Sibiu

Recipes taught: Romanian classics like Mici (grilled meat rolls), Zacuscă (vegetable spread), and Papanași (cheese doughnuts)
Duration: 2-3 hours
Cost: Approximately 180-220 RON (€36-44) per person

3. Taste Transilvania
Address: Strada Memorandumului 9, Cluj-Napoca
Recipes taught: A mix of traditional and modern Romanian cuisine, including Ciorbă (sour soup), Plăcintă (savory pie), and reinvented local desserts
Duration: 4 hours
Cost: About 250-300 RON (€50-60) per person

4. Sighișoara Cooking Workshop
Address: Str. Bastionului 8, Sighișoara
Recipes taught: Focuses on medieval Transylvanian recipes, including various meat dishes, vegetable sides, and traditional desserts
Duration: 3 hours
Cost: Around 200 RON (€40) per person

General tips for markets and cooking classes:

- Markets are typically busiest and have the best selection early in the morning.
- Bring cash to the markets; many vendors don't accept cards.
- For cooking classes, book in advance, especially during peak tourist season.
- Most cooking classes include eating the meal you prepare and often a glass of local wine.
- Don't hesitate to ask vendors or cooking instructors about the history and cultural significance of ingredients or dishes.

I found that exploring the food markets and taking cooking classes provided a deep dive into Transylvanian culinary culture. It's a great way to interact with locals and learn about the region's rich gastronomic heritage.

CHAPTER 8. Accommodation Guide

Luxury Hotels and Resorts

1. Castel Daniel (Tălişoara, Covasna County)

Address: DJ121A, Tălişoara 527135
How to get there: I drove from Braşov, which took about 1.5 hours. You can also take a train to Sfântu Gheorghe and then a taxi (about 30 minutes, 100-150 RON).
Cost of lodging: €150-300 per night

This 17th-century castle-turned-hotel offers a truly unique experience. The rooms blend historic charm with modern luxury. I enjoyed their spa facilities and the guided tour of the castle grounds.

Features:
- Gourmet restaurant serving local cuisine
- Wellness center with indoor pool and sauna
- Horseback riding and archery lessons
Family specials: They offer family rooms and can arrange kid-friendly activities like treasure hunts in the castle.

2. Teleferic Grand Hotel (Poiana Braşov)

Address: Strada Poiana Soarelui 243, Poiana Braşov
How to get there: I took a taxi from Braşov (about 30 minutes, 60-80 RON). There's also a regular bus service.
Cost of lodging: €120-250 per night

This modern resort is perfect for both winter sports and summer mountain getaways. The views of the Carpathian Mountains are breathtaking.

Features:
- Large spa complex with indoor and outdoor pools
- Multiple restaurants and bars
- Ski-in/ski-out access in winter
Family specials: Kids' club, family rooms, and special children's menus in the restaurants.

3. InterContinental Athénée Palace Bucharest

Address: Strada Episcopiei 1-3, Bucharest
How to get there: While not in Transylvania, it's a great starting point. I took a taxi from Bucharest Airport (20-30 minutes, about 50 RON).
Cost of lodging: €150-300 per night

This historic luxury hotel in Romania's capital offers a great base for exploring Transylvania.

Features:
- Multiple high-end restaurants and bars
- Health club with indoor pool

- Concierge service for arranging Transylvania tours
Family specials: Babysitting service, family rooms available

4. Hilton Sibiu
Address: Strada Padurea Dumbrava 1, Sibiu
How to get there: I took a taxi from Sibiu Airport (about 15 minutes, 30-40 RON).
Cost of lodging: €100-200 per night

Set near the Dumbrava Forest, this hotel offers a mix of city access and natural beauty.

Features:
- Large spa with indoor and outdoor pools
- Tennis courts and fitness center
- Restaurant with panoramic forest views
Family specials: Children's pool, playground, and family package deals

5. Grand Hotel Napoca (Cluj-Napoca)

Address: Strada Octavian Goga 1, Cluj-Napoca
How to get there: I walked from the city center (about 15 minutes). Taxis from the airport take about 20 minutes and cost around 30 RON.
Cost of lodging: €80-150 per night

While not the most luxurious, it offers great value and a convenient location for exploring Cluj-Napoca and surrounding areas.

Features:
- Panoramic restaurant with city views
- Fitness center and sauna
- Conference facilities
Family specials: Family rooms available, children under 12 stay free with parents

General tips for luxury stays in Transylvania:
- Book well in advance, especially for unique properties like Castel Daniel
- Many luxury hotels can arrange private tours of local attractions
- Don't hesitate to ask the concierge for recommendations - they often have great local knowledge
- Some hotels offer helicopter transfers from major cities, which can be a spectacular way to see the landscape (though quite expensive)

Remember, prices can vary significantly depending on the season. Summer (June-August) and the Christmas/New Year period tend to be the most expensive. Booking in shoulder seasons (April-May or September-October) can often get you luxury accommodation at better rates while still enjoying good weather.

Boutique Hotels and Guesthouses

I'm excited to share my experiences with some of the best boutique hotels and guesthouses in the region. Here's a guide to help you plan your stay:

1. Casa cu Zorele (Sighișoara)
Address: Str. Bastionului 11, Sighișoara 545400
How to get there: Located within the citadel walls. From the train station, it's a 15-minute walk or a short taxi ride (about 15 RON / €3).

Cost of lodging: €60-100 per night
Features:
- Beautifully restored 17th-century building
- Traditional Transylvanian decor with modern amenities
- Stunning views of the citadel
- On-site restaurant serving local cuisine
Family/kids special: Family rooms available, children under 6 stay free

2. Copsamare Guesthouses (Copșa Mare, near Sibiu)
Address: Copșa Mare 161, Sibiu County
How to get there: 60 km from Sibiu. Best reached by car (1-hour drive). Car rental from Sibiu airport costs around €30-40 per day.

Cost of lodging: €80-120 per night
Features:
- Restored Saxon houses in a picturesque village
- Farm-to-table dining experiences
- Bicycle rentals for exploring the countryside
- Traditional bread-making and jam-making workshops

Family/kids special: Kids' play area in the garden, family cooking classes available

3. Akasha Wellness Retreat (Peștera, near Brașov)
Address: Peștera 219, Brașov County
How to get there: 35 km from Brașov. Accessible by car (40-minute drive) or shuttle service from Brașov (around €20 per person).

Cost of lodging: €100-150 per night
Features:
- Yoga and meditation classes
- Vegetarian and vegan cuisine
- Spa treatments and outdoor hot tub
- Stunning mountain views
Family/kids special: Family yoga sessions, nature walks for kids

4. Zabola Estate (Zabola, Covasna County)
Address: Zabola 492, Covasna County
How to get there: 220 km from Bucharest. Best reached by car (3.5-hour drive). Private transfer can be arranged for about €150.

Cost of lodging: €120-200 per night
Features:
- Luxurious rooms in a restored castle and surrounding buildings
- Vast private forest with hiking and wildlife watching opportunities
- Farm-to-table dining
- Outdoor activities like horseback riding and carriage rides
Family/kids special: Kids' playground, family picnics in the forest

5. Miklosvar Guesthouses (Miklósvár, Covasna County)
Address: Miklósvár 186, Covasna County
How to get there: 200 km from Bucharest. Accessible by car (3-hour drive) or train to Sfântu Gheorghe, then a 30-minute taxi ride (about €20).

Cost of lodging: €70-110 per night
Features:
- Restored traditional Szekler houses
- Home-cooked meals using local ingredients
- Cultural experiences like traditional craft workshops
- Bear watching excursions in nearby forests
Family/kids special: Family rooms available, kids' activities like farm visits and pony rides

6. Viscri 125 (Viscri, Brașov County)
Address: Viscri 125, Brașov County
How to get there: 80 km from Brașov. Best reached by car (1.5-hour drive).

Cost of lodging: €90-130 per night
Features:
- Beautifully restored Saxon houses in a UNESCO World Heritage village
- Traditional Transylvanian furnishings
- Organic garden and orchard
- Workshops on traditional crafts and cooking
Family/kids special: Family suites available, kids can participate in gardening activities

General tips:
- Book in advance, especially for summer months (June-August) as these unique accommodations fill up quickly.

- Many of these places offer airport/train station pickup services, which can be convenient but more expensive than public transport.
- Some guesthouses have minimum stay requirements, especially during peak season.
- Most offer free Wi-Fi, but it's worth checking if this is important to you, as some remote locations may have limited connectivity.
- Many of these accommodations can help arrange local experiences and tours, often at better rates than you'd find independently.

These boutique hotels and guesthouses offer a unique and intimate way to experience Transylvanian hospitality. From restored historical buildings to wellness retreats, there's something to suit every taste and budget. Remember, part of the charm of these places is their rural location, so be prepared for a bit of an adventure getting there – it's all part of the Transylvanian experience!

Budget-Friendly Options

As a budget-conscious traveler, I've explored various affordable accommodations across Transylvania. Here's a guide to some of the best budget-friendly options I've encountered:

1. Burg Hostel (Brașov)
Address: Str. Apollonia Hirscher 8, Brașov 500025
How to get there: Located in the old town, a 15-minute walk from the train station or a short bus ride (2 RON / €0.40).

Cost of lodging: Dorm beds €10-15, Private rooms €30-40
Features:

- Central location near the main square
- Free walking tours
- Fully equipped kitchen
- Social common area with games
Family/kids special: Private family rooms available

2. Retro Hostel (Cluj-Napoca)
Address: Str. Iuliu Maniu 26, Cluj-Napoca 400095
How to get there: 10-minute walk from the train station, or take bus 8 (2 RON / €0.40).

Cost of lodging: Dorm beds €12-18, Private rooms €35-45
Features:
- Quirky retro decor
- Rooftop terrace with city views
- Free breakfast
- Bike rental available
Family/kids special: Board games and movie nights

3. Central Spot Apartments (Sibiu)
Address: Str. Nicolae Bălcescu 4, Sibiu 550159
How to get there: 15-minute walk from the train station, or a short taxi ride (about 10 RON / €2).

Cost of lodging: Studio apartments €40-60
Features:
- Self-catering facilities
- Central location near Piața Mare
- Modern, clean interiors
Family/kids special: Extra beds for children available at no additional cost

4. Pensiunea Casa Medievală (Sighișoara)
Address: Str. Bastionului 3, Sighișoara 545400

How to get there: Within the citadel, a 20-minute uphill walk from the train station or a short taxi ride (about 15 RON / €3).

Cost of lodging: Double rooms €35-50
Features:
- Traditional decor in a historic building
- Beautiful views of the citadel
- Breakfast included
Family/kids special: Family rooms available, playground nearby

5. Camping Zărneşti (near Piatra Craiului National Park)
Address: Str. Tohaniţa 24, Zărneşti 505800
How to get there: Bus from Braşov to Zărneşti (1 hour, 7 RON / €1.40), then a 15-minute walk.

Cost of lodging: Tent pitches €5-8, Basic cabins €20-30
Features:
- Beautiful mountain setting
- Shared kitchen and barbecue areas
- Ideal base for hiking
Family/kids special: Large grassy areas for play, nearby bear sanctuary

6. Transylvania Hostel (Alba Iulia)
Address: Str. Vasile Goldiş 1A, Alba Iulia 510007
How to get there: 10-minute walk from the bus station, or a short taxi ride (about 10 RON / €2).

Cost of lodging: Dorm beds €12-15, Private rooms €30-40
Features:
- Located near the impressive Alba Carolina Citadel
- Free city tours
- Cozy common area with books and games

Family/kids special: Family rooms available, outdoor play area

General tips for budget accommodation in Transylvania:
- Prices often increase in peak season (June-August), book in advance for better rates.
- Many hostels and guesthouses offer discounts for longer stays.
- Look for accommodations that include breakfast to save on food costs.
- Consider staying in smaller towns or villages for lower prices, especially if you have a car.
- Many budget accommodations offer free walking tours or can connect you with local, affordable experiences.
- Public transportation in Romania is generally very affordable, so don't be afraid to stay a bit further from the center if it means significant savings.
- Some hostels have age limits, so if you're traveling with family, double-check their policies.
- Consider Couchsurfing for extremely budget-friendly options, though availability can be limited.

Remember, while these options are budget-friendly, they still offer a comfortable base for exploring Transylvania. Many are centrally located, allowing you to save on transportation costs. Don't be afraid to chat with staff or other travelers - they often have great tips for free or low-cost activities in the area!

Unique Stays (Castles, Treehouses, etc.)

Transylvania offers some truly unique accommodation options. Here's my guide to some of the most interesting places I've stayed or researched:

1. Bran Castle (Dracula's Castle)
Location: Strada General Traian Moșoiu 24, Bran 507025
How to get there: 30 km from Brașov. Take a bus from Brașov (1 hour, ~10 RON / €2) or taxi (30 minutes, ~100 RON / €20).

Cost of lodging: €260-350 per night (only available on certain dates)
Features:
- Stay in the actual Bran Castle, associated with the Dracula legend
- Private guided tour of the castle
- Gourmet dinner in the castle's old customs house
Family/kids special: Special 'vampire-hunting' kit for kids

2. Sesuri Treehouse
Location: Near Șimon village, Brașov County
How to get there: 45 km from Brașov. Best reached by car (1-hour drive). Car rental from Brașov costs around €30-40 per day.

Cost of lodging: €100-150 per night
Features:
- Eco-friendly treehouse with panoramic mountain views
- Outdoor terrace and barbecue area
- Nearby hiking trails
Family/kids special: Treasure hunt activity in the surrounding forest

3. Zabola Estate - Machine House
Location: Zăbala 492, Covasna County
How to get there: 220 km from Bucharest. Best reached by car (3.5-hour drive). Private transfer can be arranged for about €150.

Cost of lodging: €150-200 per night
Features:
- Unique accommodation in a converted machine house on a castle estate
- Access to vast private forests
- Outdoor activities like horse riding and carriage tours
Family/kids special: Kids' playground, family picnics in the forest

4. Maldar Guesthouse - Gypsy Caravan
Location: Măldar 175, Alba County
How to get there: 120 km from Cluj-Napoca. Best reached by car (2-hour drive).

Cost of lodging: €50-80 per night
Features:
- Stay in an authentic, renovated Gypsy caravan
- Traditional Romanian farm experience
- Home-cooked meals using farm produce
Family/kids special: Interaction with farm animals, hayride experiences

5. Ice Hotel at Bâlea Lake (seasonal, usually December-March)
Location: Bâlea Lake, Făgăraş Mountains
How to get there: 77 km from Sibiu. Take a cable car from Bâlea Cascadă (€20 round trip). In winter, the cable car is the only access.

Cost of lodging: €100-150 per night
Features:
- Unique hotel rebuilt from ice each winter
- Ice bar and ice restaurant
- Igloo-building workshops

Family/kids special: Snow tubing activities for kids

6. Medieval Apartments in Sighişoara Citadel
Location: Piaţa Cetăţii 12, Sighişoara 545400
How to get there: In the heart of Sighişoara's citadel. From the train station, it's a 15-minute walk or short taxi ride (about 15 RON / €3).

Cost of lodging: €80-120 per night
Features:
- Stay in a 16th-century building within the UNESCO-listed citadel
- Period furnishings with modern amenities
- Central location for exploring the medieval town
Family/kids special: Medieval costume rental for kids

7. Count Kálnoky's Estate
Location: Micloşoara 186, Covasna County
How to get there: 200 km from Bucharest. Accessible by car (3-hour drive) or train to Sfântu Gheorghe, then a 30-minute taxi ride (about €20).

Cost of lodging: €120-180 per night
Features:
- Restored 17th-century country estate
- Traditional Transylvanian furnishings
- Horse-drawn carriage rides
- Bear watching in nearby forests
Family/kids special: Archery lessons, horse riding for kids

General tips:
- These unique stays often book up far in advance, especially for summer and holiday periods. Early reservation is highly recommended.

- Many of these accommodations are in rural areas with limited public transport. Having a car or arranging private transfers is often necessary.
- Some of these stays (like the Ice Hotel) are seasonal, so check operating dates when planning your trip.
- While these accommodations offer unique experiences, they may not always have all the amenities of standard hotels. Check what's provided before booking.
- Many of these places offer special packages or experiences. It's worth inquiring about these when booking.

These unique stays offer unforgettable experiences that go beyond just a place to sleep. They provide a chance to immerse yourself in Transylvania's rich history, culture, and natural beauty. Whether you're sleeping in a castle, a treehouse, or an ice hotel, these accommodations are sure to make your trip to Transylvania truly special!

CHAPTER 9. Practical Information

Visa Requirements

As someone who's navigated the visa requirements for Transylvania (which, as part of Romania, follows Romanian visa policies), I can share the following information:

EU/EEA/Swiss Citizens:
- No visa required
- Can enter with a valid national ID card or passport
- Can stay for up to 90 days in any 180-day period

US, Canadian, Australian, and New Zealand Citizens:
- No visa required for stays up to 90 days in any 180-day period
- Must have a valid passport with at least 6 months validity beyond intended stay

UK Citizens:
- As of 2024, no visa required for stays up to 90 days in any 180-day period
- Must have a valid passport with at least 6 months validity beyond intended stay

Other Nationalities:
- Check the Romanian Ministry of Foreign Affairs website for specific requirements
- Many countries require a Schengen visa or a Romanian short-stay visa

For those who need a visa:
1. Apply at the Romanian embassy or consulate in your home country
2. Processing time is usually 10-14 days, but can take up to 30 days
3. Cost varies but is typically around €60 for a short-stay visa

Required documents generally include:
- Valid passport
- Completed visa application form
- Passport-sized photos
- Proof of accommodation in Romania
- Proof of sufficient funds
- Travel insurance
- Return ticket or proof of onward travel

Important notes:
- Romania is not yet part of the Schengen Area, but is working towards joining
- A Schengen visa does not automatically grant entry to Romania
- However, holders of dual or multiple entry Schengen visas can enter Romania for up to 90 days

For longer stays or work purposes:
- Different visas and permits are required
- These usually need to be arranged before arrival

Always check the latest information before traveling, as visa requirements can change. The Romanian Ministry of Foreign Affairs website is the most up-to-date source for visa information.

Remember, while I strive for accuracy, visa requirements can be complex and subject to change. It's always best to verify this information with official sources when planning your trip.

Currency and Money Matters

Currency:
The official currency in Romania, including Transylvania, is the Romanian Leu (RON), plural Lei.

Exchange Rates (as of my last update):
- 1 EUR ≈ 4.9 RON
- 1 USD ≈ 4.5 RON
- 1 GBP ≈ 5.7 RON

Note: Exchange rates can fluctuate, so it's best to check current rates before your trip.

Money Exchange:
1. Banks: Offer good rates but may have limited hours.
2. Exchange offices: Widely available in cities and tourist areas. Look for "Schimb Valutar" signs.
3. ATMs: Widely available in cities and towns. Usually the most convenient option.
4. Hotels: Often offer exchange services but at less favorable rates.

Tips for exchanging money:
- Avoid exchanging at airports or train stations, as rates are usually poor.
- Always count your money before leaving the exchange office.
- Keep exchange receipts in case you need to exchange Lei back to your home currency.

Using Cards:
- Major credit and debit cards (Visa, Mastercard) are widely accepted in cities and tourist areas.
- Smaller towns, rural areas, and traditional markets may be cash-only.
- Inform your bank of your travel plans to avoid card blocks.
- Look for cards with no foreign transaction fees for the best rates.

ATMs:
- Widely available in cities and larger towns.
- May be scarce in rural areas, so plan ahead.
- Prefer bank-operated ATMs over standalone ones for security.
- Daily withdrawal limits may apply.

Tipping:
- Not mandatory but becoming more common, especially in tourist areas.
- Restaurants: 5-10% is typical if service charge isn't included.
- Taxis: Rounding up the fare is common.
- Tour guides: 5-10% of tour cost is appreciated.

Prices and Budget:
- Transylvania is generally affordable compared to Western Europe.
- Budget per day (approximate):
  - Budget traveler: 150-250 RON (€30-50)
  - Mid-range: 250-500 RON (€50-100)
  - Luxury: 500+ RON (€100+)

Money-Saving Tips:
1. Use public transportation where possible.
2. Eat at local restaurants rather than tourist-oriented ones.

3. Visit museums on free days (often the first Sunday of the month).
4. Stay in guesthouses or hostels instead of hotels.
5. Buy groceries from local markets for some meals.

Safety:
- Romania is generally safe, but take normal precautions against pickpocketing in tourist areas.
- Use ATMs in well-lit, secure locations.
- Avoid changing money with individuals on the street.

Tax Refunds:
- If you're a non-EU resident, you can claim VAT refunds on certain purchases over 250 RON. Look for "Tax Free" signs in shops.

Mobile Payments:
- Becoming more common in urban areas. Apps like Apple Pay and Google Pay are accepted in some places.

It's always a good idea to have some cash on hand, especially when traveling to rural areas or smaller towns. However, in cities like Cluj-Napoca, Brașov, or Sibiu, you'll find that card payments are widely accepted.

Remember, financial services and ATMs may be limited in smaller villages or remote areas, so plan accordingly if you're venturing off the beaten path. With a mix of cash and card payments, you should be well-prepared for your Transylvanian adventure!

Language Tips

Here are some helpful language tips for travelers visiting Transylvania:

1. Official Language:
The official language of Romania, including Transylvania, is Romanian. However, in some parts of Transylvania, Hungarian is also widely spoken due to the region's historical and cultural ties with Hungary.

2. Basic Romanian Phrases:
- Hello: "Bună ziua" (boo-nuh zee-wah)
- Goodbye: "La revedere" (lah reh-veh-deh-reh)
- Please: "Vă rog" (vuh rohg)
- Thank you: "Mulţumesc" (mool-tsoo-mesk)
- Yes: "Da" (dah)
- No: "Nu" (noo)
- Excuse me: "Scuzaţi-mă" (skoo-zah-tsee muh)
- Do you speak English?: "Vorbiţi engleză?" (vor-beats en-gle-zuh)
- I don't understand: "Nu înţeleg" (noo in-tse-leg)
- Where is...?: "Unde este...?" (oon-de es-te)

3. Pronunciation Tips:
- "ă" is pronounced like the 'u' in "butter"
- "ţ" is pronounced like 'ts' in "cats"
- "ş" is pronounced like 'sh' in "shop"
- "î" or "â" is a deep "ih" sound, pronounced in the back of the throat

4. Language in Different Regions:
- In the Szekler Land (parts of Harghita, Covasna, and Mureş counties), Hungarian is widely spoken alongside Romanian.
- In some Saxon towns (like parts of Sibiu or Braşov counties), you might still find some German speakers, especially among older generations.

5. English Usage:
- English is widely spoken in tourist areas, especially by younger people.
- In larger cities and popular tourist destinations, you'll often find English-speaking staff in hotels, restaurants, and attractions.
- In rural areas, English might be less common, so having a few Romanian phrases handy can be very helpful.

6. Menu Tips:
- "Meniu" = Menu
- "Mic dejun" = Breakfast
- "Prânz" = Lunch
- "Cină" = Dinner
- "Supă" = Soup
- "Carne" = Meat
- "Peşte" = Fish
- "Vegetarian" = Vegetarian

7. Signs and Directions:
- "Intrare" = Entrance
- "Ieşire" = Exit
- "Deschis" = Open
- "Închis" = Closed
- "Toaletă" = Toilet
- "Informaţii" = Information

8. Numbers:
- 1 = unu, 2 = doi, 3 = trei, 4 = patru, 5 = cinci
- 6 = șase, 7 = șapte, 8 = opt, 9 = nouă, 10 = zece

9. Cultural Tips:
- Romanians appreciate when visitors try to speak their language, even if it's just a few words.
- It's polite to greet people when entering small shops or when beginning a conversation.

10. Language Learning Resources:
- Consider downloading a language app like Duolingo or Google Translate before your trip.
- Pocket phrase books can be handy, especially in areas with limited internet connectivity.

Remember, even if you make mistakes, locals usually appreciate the effort to speak their language. Don't be afraid to try out your Romanian – it's a great way to connect with people and enhance your travel experience in Transylvania!

Health and Safety

As someone who has traveled through Transylvania, I can share some insights on health and safety considerations for visitors. Overall, Transylvania is a relatively safe destination, but it's always wise to take precautions. Here's what you should know:

Health:

1. Healthcare facilities:
   - Major cities like Cluj-Napoca, Brașov, and Sibiu have modern hospitals and clinics.

- Rural areas may have limited medical facilities.
- It's advisable to have travel insurance that covers medical emergencies.

2. Vaccinations:
   - No special vaccinations are required, but ensure your routine vaccinations are up to date.
   - Consider a tick-borne encephalitis vaccine if planning extensive outdoor activities.

3. Tap water:
   - Generally safe to drink in cities, but bottled water is widely available and recommended for sensitive stomachs.

4. Food safety:
   - Most restaurants maintain good hygiene standards.
   - Be cautious with street food and ensure meat is well-cooked.

5. Pharmacies:
   - Widely available in cities and towns, often marked with a green cross.
   - Many medications are available over the counter.

Safety:

1. Crime:
   - Violent crime rates are low, but petty theft can occur in tourist areas.
   - Be aware of your surroundings and keep valuables secure.

2. Road safety:
   - Roads can be in poor condition, especially in rural areas.

- Driving can be aggressive; if renting a car, drive defensively.
- Use licensed taxis or ride-sharing apps in cities.

3. Wildlife:
- Transylvania has a significant bear population. In rural areas, hike in groups and make noise to avoid surprises.
- Never approach or feed wild animals.

4. Natural hazards:
- In winter, be prepared for snow and ice, especially in mountainous areas.
- During summer, protect against sunburn and heat exhaustion.

5. Emergency numbers:
- 112 is the universal emergency number for police, fire, and ambulance.

6. Scams:
- Be cautious of overly friendly strangers offering unsolicited help or deals.
- Use official tourist information centers for guidance.

7. LGBTQ+ travelers:
- While attitudes are improving, some conservatism remains. Discretion is advised in rural areas.

8. Solo female travelers:
- Generally safe, but standard precautions apply, especially at night.

Cultural sensitivities:

1. Respect religious sites and dress modestly when visiting churches.
2. Ask permission before photographing people, especially in rural areas.
3. Tipping is customary in restaurants and for services.

By staying aware and taking basic precautions, most travelers find Transylvania to be a safe and welcoming destination. Remember to respect local customs and the environment, and you're sure to have a wonderful experience exploring this fascinating region.

Internet and Communication

As a traveler who's spent time in Transylvania, I can share my experiences with internet and communication in the region. Overall, I found connectivity to be quite good, especially in urban areas. Here's a breakdown:

Internet Access:

1. Wi-Fi:
    - Widely available in hotels, guesthouses, cafes, and restaurants in cities and towns.
    - Many public spaces in larger cities (Cluj-Napoca, Brașov, Sibiu) offer free Wi-Fi.
    - Quality and speed are generally good in urban areas.

2. Mobile Data:
    - 4G coverage is extensive across most of Transylvania.
    - 5G is available in major cities, though coverage is still expanding.

3. Internet Cafes:
- Less common now, but still found in some cities, often doubling as gaming centers.

Mobile Phone Services:

1. Major providers:
- Orange, Vodafone, and Digi are the main operators.
- I found Digi to offer good value for short-term visitors.

2. Prepaid SIM cards:
- Easily available at airports, provider shops, and some convenience stores.
- Bring your passport for registration.
- Costs: Around 5-10 EUR for a SIM with decent data allowance.

3. Roaming:
- If you're from the EU, you can usually use your home plan without extra charges.
- For non-EU visitors, check with your provider about roaming packages.

Staying Connected:

1. Apps:
- WhatsApp and Facebook Messenger are widely used for communication.
- Uber and Bolt work well for ride-hailing in larger cities.

2. VoIP services:
- Skype, Zoom, and other VoIP services work well where there's good Wi-Fi.

3. Social Media:
   - All major platforms are accessible without restrictions.

Postal Services:

1. Post offices:
   - Found in all towns and cities.
   - Main post offices in larger cities often have longer hours.

2. Sending postcards/packages:
   - Reliable but can be slow for international mail.
   - Private courier services like DHL and FedEx are available in larger cities for faster delivery.

Language and Communication:

1. English proficiency:
   - Widely spoken in the tourism industry and among younger people in cities.
   - Less common in rural areas and among older generations.

2. Translation apps:
   - Google Translate works well for Romanian. I found it helpful in more remote areas.

3. Learning basic Romanian:
   - A few simple phrases go a long way in making connections with locals.

Tips:

1. Download offline maps (like Google Maps) before traveling to rural areas.

2. Consider a portable Wi-Fi device if you need constant connectivity.
3. Keep your devices charged; power banks are useful for long day trips.
4. Be mindful of data usage if you're on a limited plan.
5. Public phones are rare, so don't rely on finding one in an emergency.

In my experience, staying connected in Transylvania was easier than I initially expected. While there might be some limitations in very remote areas, for the most part, you'll find that internet and communication services are readily available and reliable throughout your travels in the region.

CHAPTER 10. Seasonal Events and Festivals

Spring Events

Here's an overview of spring events and festivals in Transylvania, including cost information where applicable:

1. Transylvania International Film Festival (TIFF) - Cluj-Napoca (Late May to Early June)
This prestigious film festival showcases international and Romanian films.
Cost: Individual tickets €5-10; Festival passes €50-100

2. Sibiu Jazz Festival (May)
A celebration of jazz music featuring local and international artists.
Cost: Daily tickets €15-25; Festival passes €50-70

3. Sighişoara Medieval Festival (April)
Reenactments, craft fairs, and performances celebrating medieval culture.
Cost: Most events are free; Some special performances may cost €5-15

4. Transilvania International Guitar Festival - Cluj-Napoca (April)
Classical and contemporary guitar performances and workshops.
Cost: Concert tickets €10-30; Workshop fees vary

5. Brașov Marathon (May)
A major running event with full marathon, half marathon, and shorter distances.
Cost: Registration fees €20-50, depending on the race category

6. Târgu Mureș Spring Fair (April)
Traditional crafts, food, and cultural performances.
Cost: Free entry; Costs for food and crafts vary

7. Alba Iulia In Bloom (April-May)
Floral displays and gardening exhibitions throughout the city.
Cost: Free

8. Transylvania Ceramics Fair - Cluj-Napoca (May)
Showcasing traditional and contemporary Romanian ceramics.
Cost: Free entry; Costs for purchasing items vary

9. Sibiu Spring Food Festival (May)
Celebration of local and international cuisine.
Cost: Free entry; Food and drink prices vary

10. Mediaș Central European Wine Competition (May)
Wine tasting events and competition featuring regional wines.
Cost: Tasting sessions €10-30; Some events may be by invitation only

11. Brașov Spring Parade (May)
Colorful parade through the city center celebrating the arrival of spring.
Cost: Free

12. Mărțișor Festival - Various locations (March 1-8)
Traditional celebration of the coming of spring with handmade trinkets and cultural events.
Cost: Free to attend; Mărțișor trinkets typically cost €1-5

These spring events offer a mix of cultural, culinary, and artistic experiences across Transylvania. Many of the festivals have free entry, with costs primarily associated with specific performances, food and drink, or participation in certain activities. It's always a good idea to check the official websites of these events for the most up-to-date information on schedules and ticket prices, as they can vary from year to year.

Summer Festivals

Transylvania's summer festival scene is a vibrant tapestry of culture, music, and tradition that I've had the pleasure of exploring. The region pulsates with energy during these warmer months, offering a diverse array of events that cater to all tastes. Let me take you through some of the most captivating summer festivals I've encountered:

1. Sibiu International Theatre Festival (June)
Location: Sibiu
This is one of the largest performing arts festivals in the world. I was amazed by the diversity of performances, from theatre to dance, circus, and music.
Cost: Varies by event, ranging from free street performances to around 100-200 RON (€20-40) for main stage shows.

2. Electric Castle (July)
Location: Bonțida, near Cluj-Napoca

Set against the backdrop of Bánffy Castle, this electronic music festival offers an eclectic lineup and a unique atmosphere.
Cost: 4-day passes typically cost around 600-700 RON (€120-140) if purchased early.

3. Sighișoara Medieval Festival (July)
Location: Sighișoara
I loved stepping back in time at this festival, with its medieval reenactments, traditional crafts, and music performances in the historic citadel.
Cost: Many events are free, but some special performances may cost 20-50 RON (€4-10).

4. Untold Festival (August)
Location: Cluj-Napoca
One of the largest electronic music festivals in Europe, Untold transforms Cluj into a massive party.
Cost: 4-day passes start from around 700 RON (€140) if purchased early, increasing closer to the event.

5. Vama Veche Stufstock (August)
Location: Vama Veche (Black Sea coast)
While not in Transylvania proper, this laid-back rock and alternative music festival is popular with Transylvanian youth.
Cost: Usually around 250-300 RON (€50-60) for a 3-day pass.

6. Târgu Mureș City Days (June)
Location: Târgu Mureș
A celebration of local culture with parades, concerts, and food fairs. I enjoyed the mix of Romanian and Hungarian traditions.
Cost: Most events are free.

7. Căluşari Festival (June)
Location: Various locations in Transylvania
This traditional Romanian dance festival showcases the UNESCO-recognized Căluşari ritual dance.
Cost: Usually free to watch performances.

8. Székely Festival (July)
Location: Miercurea Ciuc
A celebration of Székely (Hungarian) culture in Transylvania, featuring folk dance, music, and traditional food.
Cost: Most events are free, food and crafts for purchase.

9. Transylvanian International Film Festival (TIFF) (May-June)
Location: Cluj-Napoca (with events in other Transylvanian cities)
Romania's largest film festival, showcasing international and Romanian films.
Cost: Individual screenings around 20-30 RON (€4-6), festival passes available for around 300 RON (€60).

10. Făgăraş Folk Festival (August)
Location: Făgăraş
A smaller festival celebrating traditional folk music and dance from the Făgăraş region.
Cost: Most performances are free.

General tips for summer festivals in Transylvania:

1. Book accommodation well in advance, especially for larger festivals like Electric Castle or Untold.
2. Many festivals offer early bird tickets at significant discounts.

3. Be prepared for warm weather, but also pack a light jacket for cooler evenings.
4. Local food and drink are often a big part of these festivals - don't miss out!
5. Some festivals (like Sighișoara Medieval Festival) can get crowded; arrive early for the best experience.
6. Check festival websites or social media for the most up-to-date information on lineups and ticket prices.

Summer in Transylvania offers a fantastic mix of modern music festivals and traditional cultural celebrations. Whether you're into electronic music, folk traditions, or arts and culture, you're sure to find something that appeals to you. The festive atmosphere and the beautiful Transylvanian landscapes make for an unforgettable experience!

Autumn Harvest Celebrations

Autumn in Transylvania is a magical time, filled with vibrant colors and rich harvest celebrations. As someone who's experienced these festivities firsthand, let me share some of the most exciting autumn events and harvest celebrations:

1. Sighișoara Medieval Festival (usually late September)
Location: Sighișoara Citadel
This festival celebrates the medieval heritage of Sighișoara with historical reenactments, traditional crafts, and local food.
Cost: Generally free to attend, but some special events may have a small fee (10-20 RON / €2-4)

2. Turda Wine Festival (late September/early October)
Location: Turda, Cluj County
A celebration of the region's viticulture, featuring wine tastings, folk music, and dance performances.

Cost: Entry is typically free, wine tasting packages start from about 50 RON (€10)

3. Rasnov Gastronomy and Film Festival (October)
Location: Rasnov Fortress
This unique event combines culinary delights with film screenings in a historic setting.
Cost: Film screenings usually 15-25 RON (€3-5) per show, food prices vary

4. Hora de la Prislop (first Sunday of October)
Location: Prislop Pass, Maramures
A traditional harvest celebration with folk music, dance, and local cuisine.
Cost: Free to attend

5. Sibiu Gourmet Festival (October)
Location: Various locations in Sibiu
A culinary event showcasing local and international cuisine.
Cost: Many free events, special dinners or masterclasses can range from 100-300 RON (€20-60)

6. Transylvanian Truffle Festival (October/November)
Location: Various locations, centered around Alba Iulia
Celebrating the prized Transylvanian truffle with hunts, cooking demonstrations, and gourmet meals.
Cost: Truffle hunting experiences from 200 RON (€40), gourmet dinners from 300 RON (€60)

7. Autumn Fair at ASTRA Museum (October)
Location: ASTRA National Museum Complex, Sibiu
A celebration of traditional crafts and autumn harvest, with demonstrations and workshops.

Cost: Museum entry around 30 RON (€6), most activities included

8. Apples' Night at Bran Castle (October)
Location: Bran Castle
A unique Halloween-themed event with a Transylvanian twist, featuring pumpkin carving and apple-based activities.
Cost: Castle entry plus event activities around 100 RON (€20)

9. Harvest Ball in Viscri (September)
Location: Viscri village
A traditional Saxon celebration with folk music, dance, and homemade food and drinks.
Cost: Usually free for visitors to observe, small fee for participation in meals

10. Cluj Napoca Wine Festival (October)
Location: Unirii Square, Cluj-Napoca
A showcase of regional wines with tastings, food pairings, and cultural performances.
Cost: Entry usually free, tasting packages from 50-100 RON (€10-20)

General tips for autumn harvest celebrations:

- Many events are centered around weekends, so plan accordingly.
- Smaller village celebrations might not be widely advertised but are often the most authentic experiences.
- Dress in layers as autumn weather can be unpredictable.
- Try local seasonal specialties like plum brandy (țuică), walnut cake (cozonac cu nucă), and various pumpkin dishes.
- Some events might require advance booking, especially for special dinners or workshops.

Remember, dates can vary slightly each year, so it's always good to check local event calendars when planning your trip. These autumn celebrations offer a wonderful opportunity to experience Transylvanian culture, taste local produce, and enjoy the beautiful fall scenery. Whether you're interested in wine, traditional crafts, or simply soaking up the festive atmosphere, there's something for everyone in Transylvania's autumn harvest season.

Winter Holiday Traditions

As someone who has experienced the winter holiday season in Transylvania, I can say it's truly magical. The region comes alive with unique traditions, festive markets, and cultural events. Here's a guide to some of the most notable winter holiday traditions and events:

1. Christmas Markets (late November - December)

Major cities like Sibiu, Brașov, and Cluj-Napoca host beautiful Christmas markets.

Sibiu Christmas Market:
- Location: Piața Mare (Large Square)
- Cost: Free entry
- Features: Over 100 stalls selling crafts, food, and mulled wine
- Special events: Ice skating rink (around 10 RON / €2 per hour)

Brașov Christmas Market:
- Location: Piața Sfatului (Council Square)
- Cost: Free entry
- Features: Traditional food, local crafts, carolers

- Special event: New Year's Eve concert (free)

2. St. Nicholas Day (December 6th)

This is when children receive small gifts in their shoes. While it's primarily a family tradition, some towns organize parades or events.

- Cost: Free to observe
- Some cities organize charity events where you can donate gifts for underprivileged children

3. Colindatul (Carol Singing)

Groups of carol singers go from house to house, especially on Christmas Eve.

- Cost: Free to participate or observe
- Some organized carol concerts in churches or halls might charge a small fee (20-50 RON / €4-10)

4. Ignat Day (December 20th)

A rural tradition of pig slaughter and preparation for Christmas feasts.

- Cost: Free to observe in villages
- Some agrotourism farms offer participatory experiences (100-200 RON / €20-40 per person)

5. New Year's Eve Celebrations

Most cities host free outdoor concerts and fireworks displays.

Poiana Braşov New Year's Party:
- Location: Poiana Braşov ski resort
- Cost: Free for outdoor celebrations, but restaurants and clubs may charge entry (100-300 RON / €20-60)
- Features: Fireworks, music, skiing, and snowboarding

6. Turca Dance (between Christmas and New Year)

A traditional masked dance performed in some Transylvanian villages.

- Cost: Free to observe in villages
- Some folklore festivals might include performances (entry fee around 30-50 RON / €6-10)

7. Târgul de Crăciun Medieval Sighişoara (Medieval Christmas Fair)

Held in the historic citadel, this event recreates a medieval atmosphere.

- Location: Sighişoara Citadel
- Dates: Usually mid-December
- Cost: Free entry, but some activities or workshops might have a small fee (10-30 RON / €2-6)

8. Winter Traditions Festival in Maramureş

While not strictly in Transylvania, this nearby region offers amazing winter traditions.

- Location: Various villages in Maramureş
- Dates: Late December

- Cost: Free to observe, but guided tours can cost 200-400 RON / €40-80 per day

9. Harghita Ice Hotel and Winter Events

- Location: Bâlea Lake, accessible by cable car
- Cost:
  - Cable car ride: about 70 RON / €14 round trip
  - Ice Hotel visit: 15 RON / €3
  - Overnight stay: starts from 400 RON / €80 per person

10. Orthodox Christmas (January 7th)

While most of Transylvania celebrates Christmas on December 25th, some communities observe the Orthodox date.

- Cost: Free to observe
- Special church services are open to the public

General tips:
- Book accommodations early, as prices can increase significantly during the holiday season.
- Many restaurants offer special Christmas and New Year's Eve menus, which can be pricier than usual (expect 150-300 RON / €30-60 per person for a festive meal).
- Public transport may run on limited schedules during holidays, so check in advance.
- Dress warmly for outdoor events – Transylvanian winters can be quite cold!

The winter holiday season in Transylvania offers a unique blend of traditional customs and modern celebrations. Whether you're exploring Christmas markets, observing rural traditions, or joining New Year's festivities, you'll find a warm welcome despite the cold weather!

CHAPTER 11. Sustainable and Responsible Tourism

Eco-friendly Accommodations

As an eco-conscious traveler, I was pleased to discover several environmentally friendly accommodations in Transylvania. Here's a rundown of some standout eco-friendly options I encountered:

1. Kalnoky's Guesthouses (Valea Zălanului, Covasna County)

Location: Valea Zălanului 1, Covasna County
How to get there: 200 km from Bucharest. Best reached by car (3.5-hour drive). The guesthouse can arrange transfers from Bucharest or nearby airports for about €150-200.

Cost of lodging: €80-120 per night
Features and services:
- Restored traditional cottages using local materials and techniques
- Solar panels for hot water and electricity
- Organic farm-to-table dining
- Guided nature walks and wildlife watching
- Traditional craft workshops
- Horse-drawn carriage rides

2. Copşamăre Guesthouses (Copşa Mare, near Sibiu)

Location: Copşa Mare 161, Sibiu County
How to get there: 60 km from Sibiu. Accessible by car (1-hour drive). Car rental from Sibiu costs around €30-40 per day.

Cost of lodging: €80-120 per night
Features and services:
- Carefully restored Saxon houses using traditional methods
- Organic garden supplying the kitchen
- Beekeeping and honey production on-site
- Cycling tours of the surrounding countryside
- Local craft and cooking workshops
- Support for local conservation projects

3. Wolves Den (Zărneşti, near Braşov)

Location: Strada Tiberiu Moşoiu 40, Zărneşti
How to get there: 30 km from Braşov. Reachable by train to Zărneşti (1 hour, €3-5), then a short walk or taxi ride.

Cost of lodging: €50-80 per night
Features and services:
- Eco-friendly construction using natural materials
- Solar and wind power
- Organic vegetable garden
- Guided hikes in Piatra Craiului National Park
- Bear and wildlife watching tours
- Volunteer opportunities at the nearby bear sanctuary

4. Cartref Eco Guesthouse (Şinca Nouă, Braşov County)

Location: Şinca Nouă 187, Braşov County
How to get there: 50 km from Braşov. Best reached by car (1-hour drive).

Cost of lodging: €60-90 per night
Features and services:
- Straw bale construction with natural plaster
- Composting toilets and grey water recycling

- Off-grid solar power system
- Permaculture garden
- Yoga and meditation sessions
- Wild foraging walks

5. Green Village Resort (Sfântu Gheorghe, Danube Delta)

Location: Sfântu Gheorghe, Tulcea County
How to get there: Accessible by boat from Tulcea (1-hour speedboat, €25-30, or 4-hour ferry, €10-15)

Cost of lodging: €100-150 per night
Features and services:
- Eco-friendly villas built with natural materials
- Solar power and water conservation measures
- Organic locally-sourced cuisine
- Birdwatching and wildlife photography tours
- Traditional fishing experiences
- Delta exploration by kayak or traditional boat

6. Szamba Guesthouse (Sâmbăta de Sus, Brașov County)

Location: Sâmbăta de Sus 442, Brașov County
How to get there: 80 km from Brașov. Accessible by car (1.5-hour drive).

Cost of lodging: €70-100 per night
Features and services:
- Traditional wooden architecture with modern eco-features
- Heating from wood biomass
- Organic farm supplying most of the food
- Horseback riding and carriage tours
- Hiking in the Făgăraș Mountains
- Traditional music and dance evenings

General tips for eco-friendly stays:

1. Many of these accommodations have limited capacity, so book well in advance, especially for summer months.
2. Some may have minimum stay requirements, particularly in peak season.
3. While most try to be accessible, their remote locations can make them challenging for travelers with mobility issues. Always check in advance.
4. These places often offer unique local experiences – take advantage of them to truly immerse yourself in the local culture and environment.
5. Be prepared for a more 'unplugged' experience – while most offer Wi-Fi, it may not be as fast or reliable as in urban hotels.

By choosing these eco-friendly accommodations, you're not only minimizing your environmental impact but also supporting local communities and conservation efforts. Each offers a unique way to experience Transylvania's natural beauty and rich cultural heritage.

Conservation Projects

Transylvania is known for its rich biodiversity and unique ecosystems, and there are several initiatives working to protect these natural treasures.

1. Carpathia Project

Location: Făgăraș Mountains, Southern Carpathians
Focus: Creating Europe's largest forested national park

This ambitious project aims to create a "European Yellowstone" in the Făgăraș Mountains. During my visit, I learned about their efforts to:
- Protect and restore forests and wildlife habitats
- Reintroduce native species like European bison
- Develop sustainable ecotourism

How to get involved:
- They offer wildlife watching tours and volunteering opportunities
- You can stay in their guesthouses, supporting local communities and conservation efforts

2. LIFE Lynx Project

Location: Various sites across Transylvania
Focus: Conservation of the Eurasian lynx

This project works to increase the lynx population and genetic diversity. I found their work fascinating, including:
- Monitoring lynx populations
- Reducing human-wildlife conflicts
- Public education and awareness campaigns

How to get involved:
- They occasionally seek volunteers for fieldwork
- You can report lynx sightings through their website

3. Apuseni Natural Park

Location: Apuseni Mountains, Western Carpathians
Focus: Protecting unique karst landscapes and cave systems

This park is a wonderland of caves, gorges, and waterfalls. Conservation efforts include:
- Sustainable tourism development
- Protection of endemic cave species
- Preservation of traditional mountain communities

How to get involved:
- Join guided eco-tours
- Participate in cave cleaning events (usually held annually)

4. Mihai Eminescu Trust (MET)

Location: Various Saxon villages in Transylvania
Focus: Cultural and environmental conservation

While primarily focused on preserving traditional Saxon villages, MET also works on:
- Promoting sustainable agriculture
- Protecting traditional landscapes
- Conserving local biodiversity

How to get involved:
- Stay in their restored guesthouses
- Participate in traditional craft workshops

5. Fundația ADEPT Transilvania

Location: Târnava Mare area, Sibiu and Brașov counties
Focus: Protecting biodiversity-rich farming landscapes

This project impressed me with its holistic approach:
- Supporting small-scale farmers
- Conserving high nature value grasslands
- Promoting sustainable rural development

How to get involved:
- Buy products from their food hub supporting local farmers
- Join their guided walks to learn about local flora and fauna

6. Rewilding Southern Carpathians

Location: Țarcu Mountains
Focus: Reintroducing European bison and restoring ecosystems

This project is working to bring back the iconic European bison:
- Releasing and monitoring bison herds
- Restoring natural grazing patterns
- Developing wildlife-watching tourism

How to get involved:
- Book a bison-tracking tour
- Stay in local guesthouses supporting the project

General tips for eco-conscious travelers:

1. Choose accommodations that prioritize sustainability
2. Respect wildlife and maintain a safe distance
3. Stick to marked trails when hiking
4. Support local communities by buying local products
5. Participate in guided tours that emphasize conservation education

During my travels, I found that many of these projects welcome visitors and offer unique experiences. By engaging with these conservation initiatives, you not only learn about Transylvania's natural heritage but also contribute to its preservation. Remember to always follow guidelines provided by the projects to ensure your visit has a positive impact on conservation efforts.

Supporting Local Communities

Transylvania has a rich cultural heritage, and there are many opportunities to engage with and contribute to local life.

1. Stay in locally-owned accommodations

I found that staying in guesthouses or small hotels owned by locals provided a more authentic experience and directly supported families.

Examples:
- Count Kálnoky's Guesthouses in Micloşoara
- Copsamare Guesthouses near Biertan
- Viscri 125 in the UNESCO World Heritage village of Viscri

Tip: Look for accommodations that employ local staff and use locally-sourced products.

2. Buy local handicrafts

Transylvania has a rich tradition of handicrafts. I enjoyed purchasing:
- Hand-woven textiles in Sighişoara
- Painted eggs in Moldoviţa
- Ceramics in Corund
- Wood carvings in Maramureş

Tip: Buy directly from artisans or certified fair-trade shops to ensure your money reaches the makers.

3. Eat at local restaurants and try regional specialties

Supporting local eateries helps sustain traditional cuisine and local farmers. I loved trying:
- Sarmale (stuffed cabbage rolls) in Cluj-Napoca
- Kürtőskalács (chimney cake) in Sfântu Gheorghe
- Cozonac (sweet bread) in Brașov

Tip: Look for restaurants that source ingredients from local farmers and producers.

4. Participate in community-based tourism initiatives

Many villages offer experiences that allow you to engage with local life:
- I joined a bread-making workshop in Crit
- Tried my hand at traditional weaving in Săpânța
- Participated in a village festival in Rimetea

Tip: Check with local tourism offices or guesthouses for community events during your visit.

5. Support local conservation efforts

Many communities are involved in preserving their natural and cultural heritage:
- I volunteered for a day with the Mihai Eminescu Trust, helping restore a Saxon house
- Joined a guided nature walk with Fundația ADEPT Transilvania, supporting their grassland conservation efforts

Tip: Even if you can't volunteer, choosing tours or accommodations affiliated with these organizations helps support their work.

6. Learn and respect local customs

Taking time to understand and respect local traditions goes a long way:
- I attended a Sunday service in a fortified church in Biertan
- Participated in a traditional hora dance in a village near Sighișoara

Tip: Always ask permission before photographing people or religious ceremonies.

7. Use local guides

Hiring local guides not only provides income but also ensures authentic insights:
- I took a walking tour of Sibiu with a resident historian
- Hired a local naturalist for birdwatching in the Danube Delta

Tip: Look for certified guides through local tourism offices or reputable tour companies.

8. Learn some Romanian

Even basic phrases are appreciated:
- "Mulțumesc" (Thank you)
- "Bună ziua" (Good day)
- "Te rog" (Please)

Tip: Language apps or pocket phrase books can be helpful.

9. Support local festivals and events

Attending local events celebrates and preserves cultural traditions:

- I enjoyed the Sighișoara Medieval Festival
- Experienced the Hora de la Prislop folk festival in Maramureș

Tip: Check event calendars when planning your trip to coincide with local festivals.

10. Be mindful of your environmental impact

Respecting the local environment indirectly supports communities:
- I used refillable water bottles to reduce plastic waste
- Chose walking or cycling tours when possible to reduce emissions

Tip: Many guesthouses now offer filtered water stations for refilling bottles.

Remember, sustainable tourism is about creating positive experiences for both visitors and hosts. By engaging respectfully with local communities and supporting their initiatives, you'll not only have a more enriching travel experience but also contribute to the preservation of Transylvania's unique cultural and natural heritage.

CHAPTER 12. Day Trips and Excursions

Nearby Attractions

1. Bran Castle (Dracula's Castle)
Location: Bran, Brașov County
How to get there: 30 km from Brașov. Bus from Brașov (8 RON / €1.60) or organized tour.
Cost of getting there: €10-20 for a tour from Brașov
Features: Gothic architecture, connection to Dracula legend, museum exhibits
Cost to visit: 45 RON (€9) for adults

2. Peleș Castle
Location: Sinaia, Prahova County
How to get there: 150 km from Bucharest. Train to Sinaia (2 hours, €10-15)
Cost of getting there: €15-20 by train from Bucharest
Features: Neo-Renaissance castle, opulent interiors, beautiful mountain setting
Cost to visit: 50 RON (€10) for adults

3. Sighișoara Citadel
Location: Sighișoara, Mureș County
How to get there: Accessible by train from major cities (e.g., 3 hours from Brașov, €10-15)
Cost of getting there: Varies, approximately €10-20 by train
Features: UNESCO World Heritage site, well-preserved medieval town, Clock Tower
Cost to visit: Most attractions require separate tickets, budget 50-100 RON (€10-20) for main sights

4. Turda Salt Mine
Location: Turda, Cluj County
How to get there: 30 km from Cluj-Napoca. Bus from Cluj (10 RON / €2)
Cost of getting there: €5-10 by public transport from Cluj-Napoca
Features: Underground theme park, salt lake, spa treatments
Cost to visit: 50 RON (€10) for adults

5. Libearty Bear Sanctuary
Location: Zărneşti, Braşov County
How to get there: 30 km from Braşov. Organized tours available (€30-40 including transport)
Cost of getting there: €10-15 by public transport from Braşov
Features: Largest bear sanctuary in Europe, rescued bears in natural habitat
Cost to visit: 60 RON (€12) for adults, guided tours only

6. Corvin Castle
Location: Hunedoara, Hunedoara County
How to get there: 100 km from Sibiu. Train to Deva (2 hours, €10), then local bus
Cost of getting there: €15-25 from Sibiu by public transport
Features: One of Europe's largest castles, Gothic-Renaissance architecture
Cost to visit: 45 RON (€9) for adults

7. Apuseni Natural Park
Location: Alba, Bihor, and Cluj Counties
How to get there: Best accessed by car from Cluj-Napoca (2-3 hours drive)
Cost of getting there: €30-40 for car rental per day
Features: Caves, waterfalls, hiking trails, traditional villages

Cost to visit: Free entry to the park, cave tours 30-50 RON (€6-10) each

8. Râşnov Fortress
Location: Râşnov, Braşov County
How to get there: 15 km from Braşov. Bus from Braşov (6 RON / €1.20)
Cost of getting there: €5-10 from Braşov
Features: Medieval citadel, panoramic views, historical exhibits
Cost to visit: 16 RON (€3) for adults

9. Viscri Village
Location: Viscri, Braşov County
How to get there: 80 km from Braşov. Best reached by car or organized tour
Cost of getting there: €40-50 for a day tour from Braşov
Features: UNESCO site, fortified church, traditional Saxon village
Cost to visit: Small fee for church entry (10 RON / €2)

10. Red Lake and Bicaz Gorge
Location: Harghita County
How to get there: 30 km from Gheorgheni. Best accessed by car or organized tour
Cost of getting there: €50-60 for a day tour from Braşov
Features: Natural dam lake, dramatic limestone gorge, hiking trails
Cost to visit: Free to explore

General tips:
- Many of these attractions can be combined into single day trips.

- Organized tours often work out cheaper and more convenient for harder-to-reach locations.
- Always check opening hours, especially for indoor attractions, as they may vary seasonally.
- Some sites offer discounts for students, seniors, or group bookings.
- Consider purchasing a multi-attraction pass in cities like Braşov or Sibiu for savings on entry fees.

These day trips offer a mix of history, nature, and culture, showcasing the diverse attractions Transylvania has to offer. Remember to plan ahead, especially for more remote locations, to make the most of your visit.

Cross-border Excursions

As a traveler who explored Transylvania and ventured into neighboring regions, I can share my experiences with cross-border excursions. Transylvania's central location in Romania makes it an excellent base for exploring nearby countries. Here's what I learned:

1. Hungary

Closest major city: Budapest (about 400 km from Cluj-Napoca)

How to get there:
- Bus: Direct buses from Cluj-Napoca to Budapest (8-9 hours, €30-40)
- Train: Overnight train from Cluj-Napoca to Budapest (10-12 hours, €40-60)
- Car: About 6-7 hours drive from Cluj-Napoca

What to see:
- Budapest's stunning architecture and thermal baths
- Debrecen, Hungary's second-largest city, closer to the Romanian border

Border crossing: Generally smooth at main crossings. EU citizens can cross with ID card; others need a passport.

2. Serbia

Closest major city: Belgrade (about 320 km from Timișoara, western Romania)

How to get there:
- Bus: Direct buses from Timișoara to Belgrade (6-7 hours, €20-30)
- Train: Connections available, but often require changes (8-10 hours, €30-40)
- Car: About 4-5 hours drive from Timișoara

What to see:
- Belgrade's fortress and vibrant nightlife
- Novi Sad, known for the EXIT music festival

Border crossing: Non-EU citizens may need a separate visa for Serbia. Check current requirements.

3. Ukraine

Closest major city: Chernivtsi (about 300 km from Brașov)

How to get there:
- Bus: Direct buses from major Transylvanian cities (6-8 hours, €20-30)

- Train: Connections available but often require changes
- Car: About 5-6 hours drive from Brașov

What to see:
- Chernivtsi's UNESCO-listed university
- The Carpathian Mountains on the Ukrainian side

Border crossing: Can be time-consuming. Non-EU citizens likely need a visa for Ukraine.

4. Moldova

Closest major city: Chișinău (about 400 km from Brașov)

How to get there:
- Bus: Direct buses from Brașov and Bucharest (8-10 hours, €25-35)
- Train: Overnight train from Bucharest (13-14 hours, €30-40)
- Car: About 6-7 hours drive from Brașov

What to see:
- Chișinău's Soviet-era architecture
- Cricova winery's underground wine city

Border crossing: Generally straightforward. Most nationalities can enter visa-free for short stays.

5. Bulgaria

Closest major city: Sofia (about 500 km from Bucharest)

How to get there:
- Bus: Direct buses from Bucharest (6-7 hours, €25-35)
- Train: Overnight train from Bucharest (9-10 hours, €30-40)

- Car: About 5-6 hours drive from Bucharest

What to see:
- Sofia's Alexander Nevsky Cathedral
- Veliko Tarnovo, the historical capital of the Second Bulgarian Empire

Border crossing: Relatively easy. EU citizens can cross with ID card; others need a passport.

General Tips:
1. Always carry your passport and check visa requirements well in advance.
2. Be prepared for potential queues at border crossings, especially during peak travel seasons.
3. If driving, ensure you have proper insurance and check if you need a vignette (road tax sticker) for the country you're entering.
4. Currency exchange: While some places accept euros, it's best to have some local currency on hand.
5. Language: English proficiency varies, so having a translation app can be helpful.
6. Public transportation options might be limited in border regions, so plan your routes carefully.

Remember, political situations and border policies can change, so always check the latest information before planning a cross-border trip. These excursions can add an exciting dimension to your Transylvania trip, allowing you to experience the diverse cultures of Central and Eastern Europe.

CHAPTER 13. Travel Itineraries

3-Day Whirlwind Tour

Here's a 3-day whirlwind tour of Transylvania that I've experienced and would recommend. This itinerary covers some of the region's highlights, giving you a taste of its history, culture, and natural beauty.

Day 1: Brașov and Bran Castle

Morning:
- Arrive in Brașov early morning (fly into Sibiu or Bucharest and take a train/bus to Brașov)
- Start with a walking tour of Brașov's old town
  * Visit the Black Church (Biserica Neagră)
  * Stroll down the narrowest street in Europe, Strada Sforii
  * Explore the main square, Piața Sfatului

Afternoon:
- Take a 30-minute drive to Bran Castle (often associated with Dracula)
  * Guided tour of the castle (about 1-2 hours)
  * Explore the castle grounds and small market outside

Evening:
- Return to Brașov
- Dinner at Restaurant Sergiana for traditional Romanian cuisine
- Take the cable car up Tampa Mountain for a night view of Brașov (if open)

Day 2: Sighișoara and Sibiu

Morning:
- Early start with a 2-hour drive to Sighișoara
- Explore Sighișoara's medieval citadel (UNESCO World Heritage site)
  * Climb the Clock Tower for panoramic views
  * Visit the Church on the Hill and the covered stairway
  * See the supposed birthplace of Vlad the Impaler

Afternoon:
- Drive to Sibiu (about 1.5 hours)
- Lunch in Sibiu's Grand Square (Piața Mare)
- Explore Sibiu's old town
  * Visit the Brukenthal National Museum
  * Walk across the Bridge of Lies
  * Explore the charming Lower Town

Evening:
- Dinner at Crama Sibiul Vechi for more traditional fare
- Night walk through Sibiu's beautifully lit squares

Day 3: Transfăgărășan Road and Peleș Castle

Morning:
- Very early start to drive the Transfăgărășan Road (about 2 hours to the start)
  * Drive one of the world's most scenic roads (open June to October)
  * Stop at Bâlea Lake for stunning mountain views
  * If Transfăgărășan is closed, visit Corvinus Castle in Hunedoara instead

Afternoon:
- Drive to Sinaia (about 3 hours from Bâlea Lake)
- Visit Peleş Castle, a stunning Neo-Renaissance castle
  * Take a guided tour of the opulent interiors

Evening:
- Return to Bucharest or your departure city (about 1.5 hours from Sinaia)

This itinerary is quite packed and involves a fair amount of driving, but it covers some of Transylvania's most iconic sights. A few tips:

1. Rent a car for flexibility, or arrange a private driver if you're not comfortable driving.
2. Book accommodations in Braşov for nights 1 and 2 to minimize moving around.
3. Purchase tickets for popular attractions in advance when possible.
4. Start early each day to make the most of daylight hours.
5. Be prepared for changes - weather can affect plans, especially for the Transfăgărăşan Road.

Remember, this is a whirlwind tour. You'll get a taste of Transylvania, but each of these places deserves more time if you can spare it in the future!

1-Week Comprehensive Visit

This itinerary assumes you're starting and ending in Cluj-Napoca, which has good international connections.

Day 1: Cluj-Napoca

- Arrive in Cluj-Napoca, known as the unofficial capital of Transylvania
- Explore the Old Town, including St. Michael's Church and the vibrant Unirii Square
- Visit the National Museum of Transylvanian History
- Evening: Dinner at Roata, trying traditional Transylvanian cuisine

Accommodation: Hotel Beyfin (around €80/night)

Day 2: Cluj-Napoca to Sighișoara

- Morning: Visit the stunning Turda Salt Mine (about 30 km from Cluj)
- Afternoon: Drive to Sighișoara (about 3 hours)
- Evening: Explore Sighișoara's medieval citadel, a UNESCO World Heritage site
- Climb the Clock Tower for panoramic views

Accommodation: Casa cu Zorele (around €70/night)

Day 3: Sighișoara to Brașov

- Morning: Visit the supposed birthplace of Vlad the Impaler
- Drive to Brașov (about 2 hours), stopping at the fortified church of Viscri en route
- Afternoon: Take a walking tour of Brașov's Old Town
- Evening: Dinner at Sergiana, known for its medieval-themed setting and local dishes

Accommodation: Bella Muzica (around €60/night)

Day 4: Brașov and Bran Castle

- Morning: Visit Bran Castle, often associated with the Dracula legend (30 km from Brașov)
- Afternoon: Return to Brașov, take the cable car up Tampa Mountain for city views
- Evening: Free time to explore Brașov's cafe scene

Accommodation: Same as previous night

Day 5: Brașov to Sibiu

- Morning: Drive to Sibiu (about 3 hours), stopping at Făgăraș Fortress en route
- Afternoon: Explore Sibiu's charming old town, including the Liar's Bridge and Brukenthal Museum
- Evening: Dinner at Crama Sibiul Vechi, set in medieval cellars

Accommodation: Artisans Boutique Villa (around €75/night)

Day 6: Sibiu and surroundings

- Morning: Visit the ASTRA National Museum Complex, an open-air ethnographic museum
- Afternoon: Drive to the picturesque village of Cisnădioara to see its fortified church
- Evening: Return to Sibiu for a farewell dinner at Jules Bistro

Accommodation: Same as previous night

Day 7: Return to Cluj-Napoca

- Morning: Drive back to Cluj-Napoca (about 3 hours)
- Afternoon: Visit the Cluj-Napoca Botanical Garden, one of the largest in Europe
- Evening: Farewell dinner at Zama, known for its modern take on Romanian cuisine

Depart from Cluj-Napoca the next day

Transportation:
Renting a car would be ideal for this itinerary, offering flexibility and easy access to rural sites. Expect to pay around €30-40 per day. Alternatively, you can use a combination of trains and buses, but this may limit your ability to visit some of the more remote locations.

Estimated Budget (per person, based on double occupancy):
- Accommodation: €450-500
- Car rental: €210-280
- Fuel: €100-150
- Food and drinks: €200-250
- Entrance fees and activities: €100-150
- Miscellaneous: €100

Total: Approximately €1160-1430 per person for the week

This itinerary offers a blend of Transylvania's medieval towns, dramatic castles, rural landscapes, and cultural experiences. It covers the major highlights while also allowing some time to soak in the atmosphere of each location. Remember to book accommodations and any guided tours in advance, especially if traveling during the peak summer season.

2-Week In-depth Exploration

As someone who's had the pleasure of exploring Transylvania in depth, I'm excited to share a 2-week itinerary that captures the essence of this fascinating region. This itinerary balances urban experiences, historical sites, natural wonders, and cultural immersion.

Day 1-3: Cluj-Napoca
- Arrive in Cluj-Napoca, the unofficial capital of Transylvania
- Explore the vibrant city center, including St. Michael's Church and the National Museum of Transylvanian History
- Visit the botanical garden and relax in Central Park
- Take a day trip to Turda Salt Mine, an otherworldly underground attraction

Day 4-5: Sighişoara
- Travel to Sighişoara (3-hour drive or train ride from Cluj)
- Wander the cobblestone streets of the UNESCO-listed citadel
- Climb the Clock Tower for panoramic views
- Visit the supposed birthplace of Vlad the Impaler

Day 6-7: Braşov
- Head to Braşov (2-hour drive from Sighişoara)
- Explore the medieval Old Town, including the Black Church
- Take the cable car up Tampa Mountain for city views
- Day trip to Bran Castle, popularly known as "Dracula's Castle"

Day 8: Sinaia
- Drive to Sinaia (1-hour from Braşov)
- Visit the stunning Peleş Castle, a masterpiece of German Renaissance architecture

- Take a scenic hike in the surrounding Bucegi Mountains

Day 9-10: Sibiu
- Travel to Sibiu (2.5-hour drive from Sinaia)
- Explore the charming old town with its unique "eyes" houses
- Visit the ASTRA National Museum Complex, one of Europe's largest open-air museums
- Enjoy traditional Transylvanian cuisine in the restaurants around Piața Mare

Day 11: Hunedoara and Alba Iulia
- Drive to Hunedoara (2-hour from Sibiu) to visit the impressive Corvin Castle
- Continue to Alba Iulia (1-hour drive) to explore its star-shaped citadel

Day 12-13: Rural Transylvania
- Head to the Saxon village of Viscri (2.5-hour drive from Alba Iulia)
- Stay in a traditional guesthouse
- Participate in local activities like bread baking or traditional crafts
- Visit the fortified church and take a horse-cart ride through the countryside

Day 14: Return to Cluj-Napoca
- Drive back to Cluj-Napoca (4-hour journey)
- Last-minute souvenir shopping and farewell dinner in the lively Piezisa Street

Throughout the trip:
- Try local specialties like sarmale (stuffed cabbage rolls), mici (grilled meat rolls), and cozonac (sweet bread)

- Sample Romanian wines, particularly those from the Târnave and Recaş regions
- Engage with locals to learn about Transylvanian traditions and folklore

Transportation:
- Renting a car offers the most flexibility for this itinerary
- Alternatively, trains and buses connect major cities, but you might need to adjust the itinerary slightly

Accommodation:
- Mix of city hotels and rural guesthouses for a diverse experience
- Book in advance, especially for popular destinations like Sighişoara

Tips:
- Be prepared for variable weather, especially in mountainous areas
- Carry cash for small purchases in rural areas
- Learn a few basic Romanian phrases - it's greatly appreciated by locals

This itinerary offers a comprehensive look at Transylvania's diverse offerings, from bustling cities to tranquil villages, historic castles to natural wonders. It allows for a deep dive into the region's rich history, stunning landscapes, and unique culture. Remember to stay flexible - some of the best experiences in Transylvania come from unexpected discoveries and interactions with the warm local people.

CHAPTER 14. Resources and Further Reading

Useful Websites and Apps

Here's a list of resources that I think you'll find helpful for planning and during your trip:

1. Official Tourism Websites:

- Romania Travel (http://romaniatourism.com/): The official tourism website for Romania, with detailed information on Transylvania.
- Visit Transylvania (https://www.visit-transylvania.us/): Focuses specifically on Transylvania's attractions and events.

2. Travel Planning and Booking:

- Booking.com: Great for finding accommodations, especially smaller guesthouses in Transylvania.
- Airbnb: Useful for unique stays in traditional houses or rural areas.
- Skyscanner: For finding flights to major Transylvanian cities like Cluj-Napoca or Sibiu.

3. Transportation:

- CFR Calatori (https://www.cfrcalatori.ro/en/): Official website for Romanian Railways, useful for train schedules and booking.
- Autogari (https://www.autogari.ro/): Information on bus routes and schedules across Romania.
- BlaBlaCar app: Popular ride-sharing platform in Romania.

4. Maps and Navigation:

- Google Maps: Works well in Romania, with good coverage of smaller towns and rural areas.
- Maps.me app: Offers detailed offline maps, great for hiking in remote areas.

5. Language:

- Google Translate: Invaluable for translating Romanian, especially in rural areas.
- Duolingo: If you want to learn some basic Romanian before your trip.

6. Local Reviews and Recommendations:

- TripAdvisor: Useful for restaurant reviews and activity recommendations.
- Yelp: Less popular than TripAdvisor but still has some good local insights.

7. Cultural and Historical Information:

- Transylvania Beyond (https://transylvaniabeyond.com/): Blog with in-depth articles about Transylvanian culture and history.
- Romanian National Tourist Office (http://www.romaniatourism.com/): Offers comprehensive information about Romanian traditions and customs.

8. Outdoor Activities:

- AllTrails app: Great for finding hiking trails in Transylvania's mountains.

- Munții Noștri (http://www.muntiinostri.ro/): Romanian website with detailed information on mountain trails and conditions.

9. Events and Festivals:

- What's On Cluj (https://whatsoncluj.com/): Keeps you updated on events in Cluj-Napoca, Transylvania's largest city.
- Sibiu Tourism (http://www.sibiu-turism.ro/): Information about events in Sibiu, including the famous International Theater Festival.

10. Weather:

- Yr.no: I've found this Norwegian weather service to be surprisingly accurate for Transylvania.
- AccuWeather app: Provides detailed forecasts for cities and smaller towns.

11. Safety and Emergency:

- Romanian Ministry of Foreign Affairs (http://www.mae.ro/en): For up-to-date travel advisories.
- Romanian Emergency Services app: Provides emergency numbers and GPS location services.

12. Local Experiences:

- WithLocals app: Connects you with local guides for unique experiences.
- EatWith app: Allows you to join local hosts for home-cooked meals.

13. Money and Budgeting:

- XE Currency app: For quick currency conversions between RON and your home currency.
- Revolut or Wise apps: If you want to avoid foreign transaction fees.

Remember to download any necessary apps and offline content before your trip, as internet connectivity can be spotty in more remote areas of Transylvania. These resources should help you plan a fantastic trip and navigate the region with ease. Enjoy your Transylvanian adventure!

Local Tourist Information Centers

Here's a guide to some of the most helpful ones I encountered:

1. Cluj-Napoca Tourist Information Centre
Address: Strada Memorandumului 21, Cluj-Napoca
Hours: Monday-Friday 9:00-17:00, Saturday 10:00-14:00
What I found useful:
- Comprehensive city maps and brochures
- Information on local events and festivals
- Helpful staff with excellent English skills
- Booking service for local tours

2. Brașov Tourist Information Center
Address: Piața Sfatului 30, Brașov
Hours: Daily 10:00-18:00
Highlights:
- Located in the historic Council Square
- Offers audio guides for self-guided city tours

- Provides information on hiking in the nearby Carpathian Mountains
- Sells the Braşov Card, which offers discounts on attractions

3. Sibiu Tourist Information Centre
Address: Piaţa Mare 16, Sibiu
Hours: Monday-Friday 9:00-17:00, Saturday-Sunday 10:00-16:00
Notable features:
- Situated in the beautiful Large Square
- Offers guided walking tours of the old town
- Provides information on the surrounding fortified churches
- Helpful for finding accommodation in the area

4. Sighişoara Tourist Information Center
Address: Strada Muzeului 6, Sighişoara
Hours: Daily 9:00-17:00 (shorter hours in winter)
What stood out:
- Located near the Clock Tower
- Offers maps of the citadel with suggested walking routes
- Information on Dracula-related attractions
- Knowledgeable staff with insights on local history

5. Alba Iulia Tourist Information Center
Address: Strada Mihai Viteazul 16, Alba Iulia
Hours: Monday-Friday 8:00-16:00, Saturday 10:00-14:00
Useful for:
- Maps and guides to the Alba Carolina Citadel
- Information on the Route of the Three Fortifications
- Details on local wine routes
- Booking for guided tours of the city

6. Târgu Mureş Tourist Information Center
Address: Piaţa Trandafirilor 5, Târgu Mureş

Hours: Monday-Friday 8:00-16:00
Highlights:
- Information on the city's Art Nouveau architecture
- Details on cultural events and festivals
- Helpful for finding local craftsmen and artisans
- Provides information on nearby nature reserves

General tips about Tourist Information Centers in Transylvania:
1. Most centers offer free maps and basic information.
2. Staff generally speak English, and often other languages like German or French.
3. Many centers can help with accommodation bookings, sometimes at discounted rates.
4. They're great sources for up-to-date information on local events and temporary exhibitions.
5. Some centers sell local handicrafts or souvenirs.
6. Many offer free Wi-Fi, which can be handy for quick online searches.

Remember, opening hours can vary seasonally, so it's worth checking in advance, especially if you're visiting outside peak tourist season. I found these centers to be excellent starting points for exploring each area, offering insights that went beyond what I could find in guidebooks or online. Don't hesitate to ask the staff for personal recommendations – they often have great tips for off-the-beaten-path experiences!

CONCLUSION

As we wrap up our journey through Transylvania, I'm reminded of the rich tapestry of experiences this enchanting region offers. From its medieval citadels and lush Carpathian landscapes to its vibrant cities and warm hospitality, Transylvania truly is a destination that captivates the imagination and leaves a lasting impression.

Key takeaways from our exploration:

1. Diverse attractions: Transylvania offers something for everyone - history buffs, nature lovers, adventure seekers, and culture enthusiasts alike will find plenty to explore.

2. Rich culture: The blend of Romanian, Hungarian, German, and Roma influences creates a unique cultural landscape reflected in the architecture, cuisine, and local traditions.

3. Natural beauty: From the Carpathian Mountains to rolling hills and forests, Transylvania's natural scenery is breathtaking and offers numerous outdoor activities.

4. Historical significance: The region's castles, fortified churches, and well-preserved medieval towns provide a tangible link to a fascinating past.

5. Modern comforts: While steeped in history, Transylvania also offers modern amenities, especially in cities like Cluj-Napoca and Brașov.

6. Accessibility: With improving infrastructure and tourism services, Transylvania is becoming increasingly accessible to international visitors.

7. Value for money: Compared to many Western European destinations, Transylvania offers excellent value, allowing travelers to experience high-quality accommodations and experiences at reasonable prices.

8. Evolving destination: As tourism continues to develop, Transylvania is striking a balance between preserving its authentic charm and catering to visitors' needs.

Some final tips for potential visitors:

- Consider visiting during shoulder seasons (spring or fall) for pleasant weather and fewer crowds.
- Don't limit yourself to the popular spots - some of the most rewarding experiences can be found in smaller villages and lesser-known areas.
- Engage with locals when possible - their stories and insights can greatly enrich your understanding of the region.
- Be open to unexpected experiences - Transylvania has a way of surprising visitors with its hidden gems.

As you plan your trip, remember that Transylvania is not just a destination, but an experience. Its landscapes, history, and people weave together to create a place that often exceeds visitors' expectations. Whether you're drawn by tales of Dracula, the allure of medieval architecture, the call of the Carpathians, or simply the desire to explore a less-traveled part of Europe, Transylvania offers a journey that's both exciting and deeply satisfying.

The region's blend of the ancient and the modern, the mythical and the real, creates a unique atmosphere that stays with you long after you've left. As you explore Transylvania, you're not just visiting a place, but stepping into centuries of stories, traditions, and natural beauty. It's a region that invites you to slow down, look closer, and immerse yourself in its many wonders.

So pack your sense of adventure, your curiosity, and perhaps a garlic clove or two (just in case!), and prepare for an unforgettable journey through one of Europe's most captivating regions. Transylvania awaits, ready to charm, surprise, and inspire you at every turn.As we wrap up our journey through Transylvania, I'm reminded of the rich tapestry of experiences this enchanting region offers. From its medieval citadels and lush Carpathian landscapes to its vibrant cities and warm hospitality, Transylvania truly is a destination that captivates the imagination and leaves a lasting impression.

Key takeaways from our exploration:

1. Diverse attractions: Transylvania offers something for everyone - history buffs, nature lovers, adventure seekers, and culture enthusiasts alike will find plenty to explore.

2. Rich culture: The blend of Romanian, Hungarian, German, and Roma influences creates a unique cultural landscape reflected in the architecture, cuisine, and local traditions.

3. Natural beauty: From the Carpathian Mountains to rolling hills and forests, Transylvania's natural scenery is breathtaking and offers numerous outdoor activities.

4. Historical significance: The region's castles, fortified churches, and well-preserved medieval towns provide a tangible link to a fascinating past.

5. Modern comforts: While steeped in history, Transylvania also offers modern amenities, especially in cities like Cluj-Napoca and Brașov.

6. Accessibility: With improving infrastructure and tourism services, Transylvania is becoming increasingly accessible to international visitors.

7. Value for money: Compared to many Western European destinations, Transylvania offers excellent value, allowing travelers to experience high-quality accommodations and experiences at reasonable prices.

8. Evolving destination: As tourism continues to develop, Transylvania is striking a balance between preserving its authentic charm and catering to visitors' needs.

Some final tips for potential visitors:

- Consider visiting during shoulder seasons (spring or fall) for pleasant weather and fewer crowds.
- Don't limit yourself to the popular spots - some of the most rewarding experiences can be found in smaller villages and lesser-known areas.
- Engage with locals when possible - their stories and insights can greatly enrich your understanding of the region.
- Be open to unexpected experiences - Transylvania has a way of surprising visitors with its hidden gems.

As you plan your trip, remember that Transylvania is not just a destination, but an experience. Its landscapes, history, and people weave together to create a place that often exceeds visitors' expectations. Whether you're drawn by tales of Dracula, the allure of medieval architecture, the call of the Carpathians, or simply the desire to explore a less-traveled part of Europe, Transylvania offers a journey that's both exciting and deeply satisfying.

The region's blend of the ancient and the modern, the mythical and the real, creates a unique atmosphere that stays with you long after you've left. As you explore Transylvania, you're not just visiting a place, but stepping into centuries of stories, traditions, and natural beauty. It's a region that invites you to slow down, look closer, and immerse yourself in its many wonders.

So pack your sense of adventure, your curiosity, and perhaps a garlic clove or two (just in case!), and prepare for an unforgettable journey through one of Europe's most captivating regions. Transylvania awaits, ready to charm, surprise, and inspire you at every turn.

Printed in Great Britain
by Amazon